To Greg & Judee :
Kindred Spirits,
friends ! Thank you
for coming into my life
Enjoy !

Maple Dale Revisited

Mary Cummings

2-6-09

Also by the author

Call Me Lydia
Maple Dale
Favored to Win
The Frog, the Wizard, and the Shrew

Soon to be released

Ellie's Crows

Maple Dale Revisited

"A Coming of Age"

~ * ~

MaryAnn Myers

Malaki, Mindy & the Whitetail Deer

Sunrise Horse Farm
11872 Chillicothe Road
Chesterland, Ohio 44026

Copyright © 2008 by MaryAnn Myers
Cover Design by Flair Graphic Arts & More

First Edition
10 9 8 7 6 5 4 3 2 1

This is a work of fiction. Names, characters, places, and
incidents either are the products of the author's imagination
or are used fictitiously, and any resemblance to actual persons,
living or dead, events, or locales is entirely coincidental.

This book is printed on recycled stock & formatted to save paper.

Library of Congress Control Number: 2008911784
ISBN: 0966878043

Sunrise Horse Farm is an organic, sustainable enterprise. It is an equine retirement sanctuary; it houses a bevy of dogs, and lives in harmony with the environment.

www.sunrisehorsefarm.net

~ 1 ~

"For all intents and purposes, Maple Dale is the same. The barns, the indoor arenas, the sand paddocks and rolling grass pastures, the cross-country course. Nothing has changed. Though known to be haunted years ago, there is almost no mention of Leah Oliver anymore. She is basically dead and gone, a thing of the past."

Mindy laughed. "Get it? A thing of the past."

"Don't even go there." Bethann shook her head. "Why are you writing that anyway?"

"For history class."

"History?"

"My history. Who wants to write about wars and memorize dates? No, not me!"

Bethann chuckled. There was fourteen years difference between these two sisters, but they were as close as twins. "Hand me that," Bethann said, pointing to the jar of saddle food.

"And look, we even have food for our saddles." Mindy tossed her the container and quickly added that historically important detail to her paper. The tack room was warm and cozy, even though it was a sinister, cold, blustery February night. Baseboard heat.

"When's your assignment due?"

"Tomorrow."

"Tomorrow?" Bethann hesitated. "And you're just starting it now?"

Mindy nodded. Bethann's occasional hesitation when speaking was commonplace. She used to stutter, and didn't now, but still had a slight hesitation in her speech every so often. "Don't worry. I'll get it done," Mindy said.

Bethann smiled. Mindy wasn't the best student in the world. Learning came easy enough, it wasn't that. According to their mother, Mindy just needed to work on applying herself.

"I know. I'll write about the hawk. Remember the hawk?" She licked the tip of her pencil and started writing. Bethann laughed. Mindy had been licking pencil tips forever. It was a habit she'd gotten into because of her constant daydreaming. She could be miles and miles away in her mind at any given moment. Then she would sense someone looking at her (her mother, her father, her teacher, or maybe Bethann) and back on task she'd appear with a quick pencil lick to show her intent. It was a habit that still sent shivers down her mother's spine even to this day, ten years after Mindy and Bethann's dad had explained to her that pencils were no longer made of lead. And while, yes, a slightly disgusting habit, it was in no way life-threatening. Double lick.

"The hawk flew into the arena early one summer morning and stayed for four days. It probably would have flown away sooner, but it crashed head-on into the glass between the arena and viewing area and knocked itself out. It fell to the ground with a thud and there it lay, flat on its back, wings spread and eyes rolled back in its head."

"Its eyes weren't rolled back," Bethann said, pointing to the last sentence.

"That was for effect," Mindy said. "Do you really think all of history is the truth, the whole truth and nothing but the truth? I think not!"

Bethann laughed. She was always laughing at Mindy.

"The hawk lay unconscious for several minutes. We thought it was dead. But then it moved its wings and we all jumped back and started screaming. That brought it around totally and it sprang to its feet."

"Sprang?"

"It did. Don't you remember? Becky thought it was chasing her." Mindy drew a breath and continued writing feverishly. "It flew around inside the arena for days and perched just about everywhere. On the mounting block, the jumps, the rafters. It had all of the horses spooked, all except for the mighty Malaki."

Bethann had to laugh again. Malaki was Mindy's horse; a ten-year old Morgan mare with an attitude.

"No one could figure out how to get the hawk to leave. We kept the arena doors open and opened all the side windows even though it was almost wintertime. We left it sweet feed to eat so it wouldn't starve, but then we went online and researched hawks and it said they only eat meat, live meat."

Mindy and Bethann had both cringed at the thought.

"A father of one of the boarders suggested it be baited with a white mouse in full view just outside the arena door, but that was voted down unanimously. No one wanted any part of sentencing a poor little defenseless mouse to sure death, without any chance whatsoever of escaping. So, the hawk just kept flying back and forth. Day three and just as we were all starting to get frantic, it flew toward the door, landed on the ground and for a moment just sat there staring out. It was so close to freedom. All it had to do was take a few steps and it would be outside, home free. Free as a bird."

Bethann laughed at the pun. Mindy, too.

"But then the hawk turned around and flew back up into the rafters and sat there for another day. Desperate, several of us decided to make a fake mouse out of cotton and material. Yolanda gave it eyes and ears and a tail, and made it look really real. Then we tied a string to it and took turns pulling it back and forth on the ground outside the arena door while we made little squeak - squeak noises."

Bethann laughed again, remembering.

"It was the squeaking noises that finally attracted the hawk in the end. One second it looked like it couldn't even see the mouse, and then the next, down he swooped. We all scattered, screaming! And when the dust settled, the hawk was gone and the fake mouse too, never to be seen or heard from again."

Mindy closed her notebook and sighed, pleased with her assignment, pleased with herself. She had a carefree life, a very good life - a sheltered life. But something was about to happen that would change all that. Something that would not only alter the course of history in Mindy's life, but the lives of everyone associated with Maple Dale, forever.

~ 2 ~

It was not uncommon to see a deer or two venture fairly close to the barns. The horses in the pasture never seemed to mind, though the deer *would* get their attention. Malaki, the most vocal of the horses, would always whinny to them. Not a hello whinny, per se. It sounded more like a commanding "what kind of horse are you?" inquiry. She'd toss her head; she loved pitching her mane and forelock up and down, always showing off. Whenever Mindy would brush her mane, Malaki would instantly shake it all back to the way she evidently preferred it, messy and wild and every which way.

Malaki whinnied again and then lowered her eyes in a penetrating gaze, ears pricked forward.

The deer stood their ground just inside the woods and stared back - two does and three fawns. The fawns were little, tiny in fact, which seemed odd, this being February. If these were last year's young, they'd be almost full grown by now. This year's crop was still months from being born. Malaki raised her head, as if annoyed these strange looking horses hadn't responded. When the deer continued to stand silently, staring at her still, she trotted up to the pasture fence and did a stomp. She loved stomping too! A stomp, a whinny, a shake of her mane and forelock. The deer took off running!

Mindy watched this all take place from the hayloft where she and her friends Becky and Yolanda had been rearranging bales of hay. A new shipment of timothy/clover mix was due to arrive today and they had to make room. Fortunately they only had about forty bales to rearrange. They'd already shifted close to thirty of them, huffing and puffing, when

Mindy got sidetracked, noticing first the deer and then Malaki's reaction to them.

"Look at her." The girls laughed. Malaki seemed indignant now that the deer were leaving. "How dare they?" Mindy mimicked her thinking. "Didn't you hear me talking to you?" Malaki ran up and down the fence line, whinnying and whinnying.

"Did you ever see deer that tiny?"

Becky shook her head. "They were sooo cute."

The girls finished re-stacking the hay then headed for the candy machine in the observation room. Bethann glanced up at them from her desk and smiled. "All done?"

Mindy nodded. It never occurred to her to mention the deer, until about an hour later, when the same five deer (or at least what looked like the same five deer) showed up again. They were even closer to the barn this time. "Bethann, look!" she whispered.

Bethann turned. "Awe...look how pretty!" The three fawns were so small. Two were twins. She could tell by the way they flanked the one doe. There was hardly any snow on the ground. There hadn't been any for about a week now, another oddity this time of year. By the same token, following an extremely dry autumn and colder than average December and January, there wasn't much for the deer to forage. The temperature this day was in the upper thirties, a heat wave.

"What do you think they eat? Mindy asked, her voice low so as not to frighten them away.

Bethann shrugged. "I don't know. What grass is left, and leaves."

"They look hungry."

Bethann had to agree. All five were much too thin.

"Maybe they're wormy."

Bethann chuckled. Mindy was quite the diagnostician of late. She offered analyses on everything. If a horse hesitated eating, "His teeth probably needed floated." If it were up to her, the dentist would have been called that day. As it turned out, that horse in particular had backed away from his feed tub because a field mouse had taken up temporary residence in it. A horse limping: "Laminitis," Mindy surmised. No, just a big huge mud clump stuck in its hoof. Cribbing: "I know why horses crib; they're lacking something inherent to their system and...."

"Maybe we should feed them," Mindy suggested, when the two does turned their heads and looked at her.

"Don't you dare! You know what Dad said."

"What? That was about the raccoons."

"Mindy!"

"Fine. I said fine! I won't feed them."

Mindy had a habit of feeding everything. She even tried feeding slugs once, thought they might like corn meal, knew whatever they ate had to be small, and corn meal was the only thing she could find in the house that small. The slugs didn't eat it. Mindy had watched them for hours. "Did you know slugs poop," she told her mom and dad at dinner that night. She was eight years old at the time. Her mother rolled her eyes. "I don't know why or how though, since they certainly didn't eat."

"Maybe they're not hungry," her dad had suggested, chuckling.

The deer grazed on dormant grass. "That can't taste good," Mindy said.

"Leave them alone," Bethann said emphatically.

~ 3 ~

Mindy managed to "not feed" the deer for most of the day. But come evening, she couldn't stand it anymore. The sun was going down and they were still hanging around. The does looked so hungry with their bellies all tucked up as they shivered. She brought out the old standby, everyone's favorite - sweet feed. She filled a bucket half full and added a little salt. She knew deer liked salt because they sold salt blocks at the feed mill for deer. Salt licks, they called them. She cut up some carrots and an apple, added a cup of bran "for their digestion" and a little flaxseed for extra measure, a dab of corn oil on top so they'd have shiny coats, and down over the hill she and Yolanda went.

The little herd of deer ran away from them.

"Oh no, don't. Come back, come back." Mindy's heart skipped a beat as she and Yolanda watched them blend into the thicket of trees and ultimately disappear, still hungry. "Let's just leave it here," she sadly suggested. "Maybe they'll come back."

"But what about the raccoons?"

"What raccoons? I haven't seen a raccoon for months now."

It was true. The raccoons were long gone, and the dreaded opossums too. Mindy's dad had taken care of that. "Don't ask," he'd said. "You don't need to know."

Mindy had refused to talk to him for days following their departure.

Yolanda climbed back up the hill behind the barn, looked one way and then the other, and waved for Mindy to follow. There was no one else at the barn at the moment, but one can never be too careful. Bethann had uncanny sensory abilities. She could see and hear things miles away it seemed. There was the time the three of them, Mindy, Yolanda and Becky were lost, they'd gotten off the trails, and....

A car pulled in and instinctively, Mindy and Yolanda dropped to the ground and backed down over the edge of the hill out of sight. For an instant, they were nine and ten years old again, playing hide and go seek. It turned out to be Mrs. Butchling, whom Mindy had nicknamed Mrs. Bitchling.

"I don't like you saying that," Mindy's mother scolded, the first time she heard the nickname.

"What? A bitch is a dog. It's not a swear word."

"Yes, but Mrs. Butchling is not a dog...so, so much for that argument."

"She does kinda look like a dog," Mindy pointed out. "An Irish Setter, don't you think?" Mrs. Butchling was really thin, had long arms and legs and a long nose, and long red hair parted down the middle that hung limp like ears on each side of her head. The woman hardly ever smiled though. If dogs smiled, Mindy pictured Irish Setters smiling all the time. The Setters she knew were always so happy, jumping up and down, wagging their tails. Mrs. Butchling was a cranky, growling old Irish Setter. Whenever she did smile, which was rare and certainly not for "children's sake," all her teeth showed, even the back ones. They listened for a car door to slam, followed by the sound of the barn door being slid open, closed, and then Mrs. Butchling's voice. "Mummy's here!" Mindy imagined her smiling at her horse, Dew Drop, and every one of her teeth showing.

Behind the girls, the deer approached the food, one by one, and ever so tentatively, the two adults first, followed in size by the three young ones. When Mindy and Yolanda turned slowly, there they were, munching, the littlest of them standing right in the middle of the feed and with a mouthful.

Job well done.

Mindy knew enough about deer to know that they moved around a lot. Their bellies would be full this evening, and tomorrow they'd be gone, searching for food elsewhere. She felt good, and yet somewhat sad. She worried where their next meal might come from, but as her dad liked to say, "Nature has a way of providing." Mindy sighed. For today at least, nature by way of Yolanda and her, had provided them a feast. Tomorrow it would be out of her hands. There was no sense naming the deer, as she'd done with the raccoons. Tiger Lilly had been Mindy's favorite, so cute and fuzzy. No, no sense naming them at all. And yet she really couldn't help herself. The longer she watched the smallest one, the more she felt the urge to connect, to introduce herself, to know its name, to give *it* a name. She'd even named her bicycles as a child, and her four-wheeler, the one that got her grounded for a week for going too far. Harvey. It was all Harvey's fault. It was too easy to pedal. She wondered if the little deer's ears were soft, she wondered if its coat felt like a horse's. Would it stand to have its hooves picked? Maybe if she trained it young enough.

Pixie Dust. She'd name the little one Pixie Dust.

"Wild animals are wild animals," she could almost hear her father saying.

She imagined the little deer frightened if she were to approach it, much the same as Malaki had been that first time. Malaki, being Malaki, often reacted aggressively when she was experiencing the unknown. She'd pin her ears, she'd take that stance. She'd even try to kick a person, bite them, if she didn't trust them. It took a long time to win her trust. The little fawn nuzzled its mom.

~ 4 ~

Mindy and Bethann's parents were in Europe celebrating their 30th wedding anniversary. The trip was scheduled for a month and they were into their second week. A letter arrived from their mother on Friday, wishing the girls well, wishing they could/would have come along. "It's supposed to be a second honeymoon, Mom." Wishing for nothing bad to happen while they were gone. Wishing for less rain. They were in London at the time. Wishing them love.

Mindy passed the letter back to Bethann. "What's for dinner?"

Bethann's husband Benjamin...no, not Ben but Benjamin, was away as well, on business, and it was just the two of them. "How about French fries and some applesauce?"

"Works for me. Do you have ketchup?" Mindy plopped herself down on the couch in the kitchen. Bethann and Benjamin lived in a huge old Victorian home in the Village of Burton, not very far from Maple Dale, and had couches everywhere; in the kitchen, the dining room, three in the living room, two in the den, one in the bedroom. There was even one in the main bathroom. A big overstuffed double recliner piled high with clothes, and a dainty Queen Anne in the foyer. Benjamin had a thing about couches, said they "Called out to him."

Mindy's favorite was the one in the kitchen. It was upholstered in chintz with a really "cool" pattern. It was a hunt scene without the fox. Bethann had upholstered the couch herself. Both she and Mindy loved the idea of riding a hunt, just not the actual hunt part itself. When Bethann had laid out the upholstery material, Mindy suggested they remove all the poor little foxes, which they did, and Bethann patched it all back together with one of Persian Sun's old wool blankets. Persian Sun was Bethann's favorite horse growing up. He lived to a ripe old age of twenty-eight, and was healthy till the day he died. He lay down in the pasture one morning, went to sleep, and that was that. Bethann had ridden him just the day before and true to his character, he was quite the handful.

Bethann's French fries weren't just any ordinary French fries. These were organic-grown Russets with the skins left on, sliced thick, fried in olive oil, and seasoned with sea salt. Mindy liked to dip hers in ketchup. Bethann ate them plain, and always, always, always had them with applesauce; the no sugar-added kind that she herself had made.

"I wish Cotton was a Monkey."

Bethann laughed. From the time she could remember, Mindy would say things like this out of the blue; a quote from a movie, television show, newspaper article, silly saying. For months last year, she walked around saying, "boogie." Why, even she didn't know. She said she just liked the sound of it.

"Do you think Mom's having fun?"

Bethann nodded. "She's probably lining all the toilet seats so as not to get germs. But having fun, yes." They both knew their dad was having fun. He'd have fun in a paper bag, their mom insisted. He worked hard and played hard whether it was tennis, golf, or racquetball. He and his son-in-law Benjamin had nothing in common. Benjamin worked,

worked, and worked. And then worked some more. "Asian philosophy," Benjamin would say, with a bow.

"How was your violin lesson?"

"All right, I guess." Mindy had started taking violin lessons two summers before just to please her mom. It was torturous in the beginning, not only for Mindy but poor Mrs. Raddison as well. Once Mindy put her mind to it and learned the basics, she found herself liking it more and more. A tomboy by nature, Mindy underwent a transformation with violin in hand. Much to her mother's delight, she became elegant, reserved, gifted. "My heart wasn't in it today for some reason."

"Why not?" Bethann passed her the plate of French fries. There were three left.

"I don't know. She said I was tiptoeing; that I was holding my breath."

"Were you?"

Mindy shrugged. "Beats me." Truth was, she was thinking of the deer - the little one in particular. Little Pixie Dust. It had a slight limp. Mindy didn't notice it the first time she saw her, or even the second. It's hard to see a "slight limp" when an animal is running, which Pixie Dust did often. Around in circles, ten feet away and then back, run, run, run...bump into her mom, then she'd run some more. But today, a little calmer when Mindy and Yolanda put down another offering of food, Pixie Dust walked right up to it. And there was the limp.

Mindy wondered what the bottom of a deer hoof looked like. She considered asking Bethann, but figured she'd get a lecture and warnings, and decided to get the information herself. "Do you mind if I use one of Benjamin's computers?"

Bethann hesitated. "Why?" Benjamin was such a stickler about his computers, all three of them.

"I need to do some homework."

No games, was Benjamin's rule. None! Zip, zilch, nada! "Sure, go ahead. I'll do the dishes."

"Thanks!" Mindy went into the den and plopped herself down in front of the Dimster, so named for the lightness of the screen. Benjamin built the computer himself, and had frequent nightmares over why and how this phenomenon occurred. He'd tried four different screens, and still, no explanation. It was just plain "dim".

Mindy tap-danced through the process of getting online, into her favorite search engine, and posed her question. "What do you know about deer hooves?"

Up came an abundance of information. She scanned the first four sites; all mentioned a hoof disease, appropriately abbreviated HD. She leaned closer and closer to the screen with each dreadful word; some were so faded she could hardly make them out. High incidences of (word unclear) epidemics (another word unclear) slogging, no, sloughing, loss of entire hoof, death. Very clear. She sat back with a shudder.

"Mindy, do you want some frozen yogurt?"

"Sure. I mean, no. Yes, I'll be there in a minute." Mindy glanced at Benjamin's main computer. It was his pride and joy, but always took forever to boot. The reason she'd chosen the Dimster, initially, was because it was so fast. She had even less time now. Stick with the Dimster. She punched in the next site - same disease, different faded words, and the next, and the next. Three to six months. Three to six months what?

"Mindy?"

"I'm coming."

Bethann glanced at her as she entered the kitchen. "What's the matter with you? Are you okay? You're as white as a ghost."

Ghost.... Death.... "I'm fine. I just hate homework, that's all." She heaved a heavy sigh. Poor little Pixie Dust. With HD, chances are she wouldn't live to see summer.

~ 5 ~

If Malaki were a person, she'd definitely be a morning person. Afternoons and evenings she could be a bit cranky. She'd pin her ears when Mindy would groom her; although normally she liked being brushed. Evenings, when Mindy would tack her and tighten her girth, she'd raise her left hind leg and not kick so much as threaten to kick, a warning kind of a kick, but a kick nonetheless. Or she'd paw, and paw and paw...and paw. If she could talk, she'd probably be saying, "Why now? I was comfortable. I was eating my hay. I'm winding down from my day, not bothering you, not bothering anyone. Why now? Why now? Why now? *Leave me alone!*"

Mindy led her into the arena. Mrs. Butchling was schooling Dew Drop "on the flat" (no jumps) at the far end. Again, most mornings, Malaki would stand like a saint at the mounting block. Evenings, Mindy would usually have to circle her around at least twice. This evening it was three times.

"You really should break her of that," Mrs. Butchling said, in that annoying nasally always-the-authority voice of hers.

"Yeah, yeah," Mindy mumbled to herself. Malaki not standing still was the least of her worries at the moment. "Someday, when I have time."

"If you don't have time now, little girl, you never will."

Mindy rolled her eyes. Another thing Malaki did differently in the evening was warm up slowly. It took forever it seemed, to get her to relax, to loosen up, to take the bit. Most riders would be practically done, and Mindy would just be getting started.

Mindy walked Malaki on a long rein, urging her to move forward, tapping her ever so softly with the dressage whip, but only after asking with her legs. "Always ask first with your legs," Bethann would say.

"But she's being so lazy," Mindy insisted.

"Not lazy. She's just not using her back. Don't you feel it?"

"No."

"You will."

Bethann had learned from the master, the legendary Leah Oliver, and often sounded just like her. "You feel, you sense." Her voice would even change whenever she repeated anything she'd been taught by Leah. It became reverent, soft....

"When she starts to lower her head, give with your hands. Yes, that's it. Now drive with your seat. Ask, ask, ask."

Malaki had an awesome extended trot. It took a half hour to warm her up for it, but once she got in stride, so to speak, it was ask and ye shall receive. She performed beautifully! But then, just when it was getting to be really, really fun, here came that Bethann-sounding-like-Leah-Oliver voice again. "There, now that's enough. That's a lot of work. She's got her hind legs up underneath her, that's very, very hard work. It's like sit-ups, takes just as much muscle control. She can only do so many. Good job. Tell her good job."

Mindy patted Malaki on the neck and stroked her mane. "You're such a pretty girl." Mindy kept Malaki's mane long; a true Morgan mane, and long forelock. She loved it, loved Malaki. "If something ever happened to you, I'd die." Ever since she'd read those website articles about HD, it was all gloom and doom, all she could think about. Deer dying, horses dying.

"Nature sucks." So many things could happen, so many dangers. There was illness and disease everywhere - people killing people, animals killing animals. War. She cooled Malaki out and phoned Yolanda from the barn. "Where are you?"

"I'll be there shortly. Bill's dropping me off." Bill was her oldest brother. He was seventeen.

"Good." She looked around, so as not to be heard. "I have everything ready." The plan was to make a mud path to the feed they'd been leaving out for the deer. Mindy needed to analyze Pixie Dust's hoof print to know for sure if she had

HD. And if so, they'd have to try and treat it. How, wasn't a concern at the moment. She first needed to make a diagnosis. Back when Mindy was ten years old, she tried to learn how to do a cartwheel. She tried so hard she made herself dizzy. "I deduce," she'd said, her head spinning. Deduce was her "word of the day" that day. "I deduce that my center of gravity must be too low. Mom, show me again."

"No. It's not good to be dizzy. You've had enough. You're making *me* dizzy just watching you." Mindy had been at it for hours. "Who cares if you can't do a cartwheel?"

"Me!"

She learned to do what looked like a glorified leapfrog instead. Down with her arms, balance for a second or two, hold it hold it hold it, kick up her feet, and over she'd go. No wheel, no cartwheel, just a sideways leapfrog. The maneuver came in handy today. When she and Yolanda were just about done spreading the mud path for Pixie Dust, they heard a noise. It was a deer, a momma one. Two perfectly executed leapfrog moves and Mindy was out of the way. Yolanda scrambled behind her. The whole herd was but five yards from them.

"Oh no...." The deer approached in single file. Mindy hadn't figured on that. How was she going to know which hoof prints were Pixie Dust's? She'd thought of just about everything else. The mud couldn't be too dry. It wouldn't leave enough of an impression. Too wet and it would probably ooze and fill back in as soon as they lifted their feet. She added a little sand for good measure and this batch of mud was deemed "just right."

She and Yolanda crouched down in the bushes, Sherlock Holmes and Watson style. Yolanda scanned high and low for spiders, bugs. "Do snakes come out in the winter?"

"No. Shhh."

One deer, two deer, three deer.... There were seven total today. Pixie Dust was the last to go through the mud. She was still limping, maybe even more so. "Is that blood?" Mindy whispered. "Do you see blood?"

Yolanda shook her head, staring so hard she had to blink every so often to keep her eyes from crossing. If Pixie Dust's hoof was in fact bleeding, they'd never know. Not today at least. When the deer finished eating, the herd turned and left by the same path, Pixie Dust and her dam leading the way. The mud, with its abundance of hoof prints - was nothing but a communal mush.

~ 6 ~

All day at school the next day Mindy fretted. She could hardly wait to get back to Maple Dale. When the time finally came, it was raining, a downpour. She and Yolanda fed the deer and hurried back into the barn, dripping wet. They'd considered taking an umbrella, but thought that might look suspicious. Umbrellas weren't cool at their "teen" age. They'd have to be "up to something" to use one. Mrs. Butchling would notice for sure.

They dried off with paper towels and climbed the ladder to the hayloft and looked out. A minute or two later up over the hill the deer emerged, right on schedule. Mindy studied them through the steady rain, as Yolanda surveyed the barn rafters, fearful of bats. There were always bats at a barn, particularly one with a hayloft this large.

"She's still limping." Mindy nudged her. "Look."

Yolanda lowered her eyes and agreed. Limping, limping, limping. The two sat down woefully on a bale of hay. "I think we should just treat her," Mindy said.

"How?"

"I don't know." Mindy rocked back and forth, the wheels spinning in her mind. "I would think that HD's a lot like thrush, no? Why don't we just treat it like thrush?"

"Oh sure," Yolanda said, scanning the rafters again. "Why didn't I think of that? We'll just pick up her feet, squirt a little iodine in, and she'll be all set."

Mindy shoved her playfully and chuckled. She felt like laughing, but the Pixie Dust situation was too grim for laughter. "How much do you have?"

"What? The iodine stuff?"

Mindy nodded.

"Half a bottle."

"Good." Mindy jumped to her feet. "I've got a whole one. Let's hurry. We'll squirt it onto the path."

Yolanda beat her to the ladder and scurried down first, almost landing on top of Mrs. Butchling. The two of them grinned sheepishly as they sidestepped past her. "What are you two up to?" the woman asked. Same thing she always asked.

"Nothing. Why would we be up to anything? It's raining, that's all," Mindy said, with Yolanda nodding. "There's nothing to do, that's all. See ya!"

The two flew into the tack room, grabbed their bottles of thrush medicine, tucked them under their coats, and headed out the barn door. "Wait," Mindy whispered. Since Mrs. Butchling had already seen them and they'd mentioned the rain, why not take the umbrella. Mindy grabbed it, popped it opened, and the two rushed outside, clutching the handle. They ran around the back of the barn, slipping and sliding, and went far enough down the deer path so as not to be seen from the barn - poured the thrush medicine on the trail in a high spot, and then scrambled to hide behind a tree.

"Maybe with the rain, they won't smell us," Mindy said.

A large doe came back down the trail first, hesitated at the sight of the iodine mixture, sniffed, and walked around it. The one right behind her did the same thing.

"Oh no…" Mindy whispered.

"They probably think that it's blood." It did look like blood, lots of blood, runny blood. The two huddled under the umbrella.

The next doe stepped into it with its right front and right hind hoof. Mindy and Yolanda held their breath. The other two yearlings trotted through it. Then it was Pixie Dust's dam's turn, no problem, all four feet - and right on her heels, Pixie Dust.

"Yes!"

Pixie Dust stopped dead in her tracks and looked in their direction.

"Oh no, she sees us." Mindy and Yolanda froze.

The tiny little deer stared at them and made full eye contact. Mindy couldn't believe it. It just stared and stared for a moment, from one to the other. Then it raised it eyes slightly above them and stared even more intently.

"The umbrella. Oh my gosh, she's looking at the umbrella."

Mindy couldn't decide whether to lower it or not. She didn't want to frighten the little deer. Its mother had stopped and was waiting for her with a rather impatient, parental look on her face.

"What should we do?" Mindy whispered, tight-lipped.

"I don't know," Yolanda said, under her breath.

No sooner said and the little deer starting walking toward them, eyes still intent on the umbrella. The girls again held their breath. Mindy watched Pixie Dust's feet as she approached - all four were thoroughly covered in the iodine mixture, tiny little steps, limp, limp...but with a very brave stance.

"Oh my gosh, she is so beautiful."

Mindy nodded. "Look at her eyes."

She was trying to blink away the rain.

"Shhhh..... Don't move."

The little deer came closer and closer, close enough to practically touch, and Mindy couldn't help herself. She extended her hand. "It's okay, we're friends," she said, softly.

Pixie Dust was within inches of her hand, head extended and curious, so close, closer...then even closer. And then it happened. She touched Mindy's hand with her muzzle, touched it and then quickly backed up. It had been the very lightest of touches, but a touch nonetheless. Then she turned and with a bound, ran to her mother and off with the others.

When the girls returned to the barn, on cloud nine and full of awe, there was a message written for them on the blackboard. "Be careful what you wish for," it read. They both recognized Mrs. Butchling's handwriting.

~ 7 ~

Typically, Malaki had days when she could be very lovable, and then a day when she didn't want anything to do with anyone; not even Mindy - morning, noon, *or* night. Today was one of those days. It was as if she couldn't stand being in her own skin. "It's her time of the month," Bethann said casually. "Don't take it personally."

"But I don't get it. I'm not mean during my time of the month. All I have is cramps."

"Yes, and you let everyone know. Mom, I don't want to go to school. Mom, can you make me hot chocolate. Dad, can you stop at Malleys? I need marshmallow! I need chocolate! Bethann, can you wait on me hand and foot?"

They both laughed. "The only way horses relate is through their body language," Bethann said. They both turned and looked at Malaki, who promptly pinned her ears. "See."

Mindy had a date that evening. Well, not a *real* date – an algebra study date. She didn't especially like the guy, not all that much anyway, though he could be funny on occasion. Besides, he was practically a relative. He was her Aunt Ginger's stepson from her third marriage. She was on her fourth. The kid's name was Howard. Howard-the-Nerd Lupinski; a fourteen-year-old genius wanna-be. Twice during the evening, Mindy wished she could pin her ears like a horse. Howard seemed to be sitting too close, and kept bumping her hand when showing her how to calculate the figures. And what's this? Was he wearing cologne? That was new.

Pi Equals Square. Chocolate pie, Mindy thought, with whipped cream. Stop crowding me. She moved her hand out of reach. $(29+q = -2(q-13)$. Mindy's mind wandered, as usual. She wasn't getting D's on her tests for nothing. Concentrate. "Concentrate, concentrate, concentrate," her mom would say. "Mindy, are you concentrating?" Yes. No. She was thinking about Little Pixie Dust.

If you interfere....

"Mindy?"

"Yes." She looked at Howard. He didn't wear glasses, but had the appearance of someone who should. His eyes always seemed to be searching for something he couldn't quite see. Not a far-away look, more like a close-up. Zoom lens.

He hesitated. "Never mind."

Pixie Dust hadn't been with the herd today at the barn. Mindy had almost panicked, but then realized Pixie Dust's dam wasn't with the herd either. It might even have been a different herd. "I wonder how deer form a herd?"

Howard looked at her.

She'd read earlier online that deer were nomads, seldom territorial. "Lest it be miles and miles of foraging in a certain area that was somehow managed by man-made barriers." Barriers, the Great Barrier Reef, she remembered thinking; the first thing that popped into her mind. Another article said they stayed within a two-mile area and....

"A herd's a herd. What's the difference?"

"I'm just wondering, how many it takes to constitute a herd?"

Howard's searching eyes lit up. Numbers, he was a numbers man. "I don't know, two or more maybe." He smiled. Mindy seemed pleased with his answer.

"I'm done. I can't think," she said, and sat back.

Howard smiled again. "As in, you were thinking before?" He closed the algebra book.

Mindy laughed. He really *could* be funny at times. "Thanks, Howard," she said, for the laugh, the lesson, the cologne - it really did smell nice. "Same time next week?"

He nodded and stood to leave. He was a big kid, unlike most nerds. He even had some muscles, now that she was noticing...and three, no, four medium-sized pimples on his face. He hesitated again, as if he wanted to ask her something. But it must not have been that important, because then he turned and left without saying another word.

Bethann threw a carrot salad together for dinner while watching Dr. Phil. She started with shredded organic carrots, added lots of raisins, organic of course, then sunflower seeds and pecans, organic – organic, mixed it all together with homemade mayo, and topped it off with some of Mindy's favorites, organic marshmallows. Along with a loaf of her hardy 7-Grain bread, hot out of the oven, this was her favorite kind of meal. She paused to watch Dr. Phil take hold of his wife's hand and exit at the end of the program. She loved that. Benjamin was due home from work soon.

Conversation at the dinner table revolved around the barn, as usual, and the animals. Benjamin was sorely allergic to both. Whenever confronted with either, he'd go into sneezing fits. He loved animals, particularly dogs, Beagles to be exact. As a child he had a Beagle puppy, but it had to be taken back to the breeder within a week, because of a severe allergic reaction that landed him in the hospital, literally gasping for breath. The oddity of this type of allergy is it didn't seem to be pet dander that affected him, just the animals themselves, their saliva maybe or their breath. Bethann's barn clothing never brought on fits, or her hair, she certainly didn't wash her hair three or four times a day, as often as she was at the barn most days. His allergy only activated when he was around the actual animals themselves. Any animal.

There was a craze a few years back, cyber-pets. Bethann got him one for his birthday, and even that brought on anxiety. It's all in your head, Bethann's father declared one day, when he brought home a stray and it too had to go, if he ever wanted to see his son-in-law again for Sunday dinners. Poor Benjamin had sneezed and coughed, wheezed, turned very pale and sneezed some more to the point of getting a nose bleed, all within a half-hour timeframe. Dogs were out, cats were out, and horses - at the barn, he could never even get out of the car.

He heard all about Bethann and Mindy's day; start to finish, from the barn up through the study date.

"Why does everyone need to know algebra anyway?" Mindy asked. Benjamin glanced at her. He was a "good doer" as they say in horse circles. He loved to eat. "Pass me the bread, please."

"I mean, who cares?" Mindy handed him the breadbasket. "I'll never use it. I'll bet once I get out of school, it'll never come up again. Why crowd my brain?"

Bethann chuckled at her sister, as well as in anticipation of what Benjamin's response might be. He and Mindy reveled in discussions like this.

"You can't crowd your brain. It won't let you. It's designed to store information like that on the back shelf, so if and when you do need it – yes, you may very well have to stop and think; now where did I leave that and you might have to go looking for it. But then lo and behold, around the corner, there it'll be, with the answers to things like - if the only numbers in a matrix are a, b, c, and d and $a + d + c + d = 0$, how do you show that the determinant of the matrix is zero?" He turned to Bethann. "God, I love your honey butter, Honey," he said, and hardly missed a beat. "Same goes for the brain's connection to dreaming. Do you know why you dream? It's to vent, to let off steam, to rid yourself of excess brain-gas."

Mindy laughed. So did Bethann.

"It's like cleaning house every night."

Bethann smiled. "Oh, so that's why I don't like dreaming! No wonder."

"Oh, but that is the beauty," Benjamin said. "You can't stop yourself. If you sleep, you're going to dream. That is how the Maker designed us. We are all dreamers." Benjamin loved dreaming. So did Mindy.

"Not me," Bethann insisted. "I never dream anymore. When I wake up, no matter what time of the night or day, my mind is a blank. Sometimes I wake up and you're talking in your sleep and I don't even know who I am. How do you explain that?"

"Easy," Benjamin declared. "It is then, that I am dreaming for you." The three of them laughed. "I never want you to do without anything," he said, and meant it.

~ 8 ~

"Yes!" Pixie Dust and her mom were back with the herd. Seeing the two of them was a tremendous relief to Mindy, Yolanda, and Becky. But sadly, the little deer was still limping, and considerably more than before. Mindy agonized and agonized and agonized, what to do, what to do, what to do. "We have no other choice. We've gotta keep treating it." They created another iodine mud path, waited for the deer to come eat, and watched.

Success. Every deer walked through it as if it were just any other old ordinary mud path, even little Pixie Dust, right on her mother's heels. Mindy smiled. This was encouraging. Sometimes a horse with thrush had to be treated weeks to rid itself of the symptoms. The girls started back toward the barn, stopped to firm up the sides of the mud path to keep the iodine from seeping out should the deer venture back this way on their own, and noticed something foreboding. The littlest hoof-print, the right front of the last deer to go through, Pixie Dust's – was indeed bloody, a different color red. They tracked the prints into the brush to be sure, where Mindy picked up a blade of grass and rubbed it against her pant leg. Yes, it was blood. More than likely, as they suspected, it had been bleeding the other day as well. The three girls looked at one another.

"We need to call a game warden," Becky suggested.

"Right, so they can send someone out to shoot her? Oh yeah, that'll work."

When Mindy touched the blood with her finger, both Becky and Yolanda screamed.

"Don't!"

"What if she has rabies?"

"Cut it out, she doesn't have rabies!" Mindy said, angry, but also just a tad frightened at the idea. "She's just got a foot disease, that's all." She wiped every last speck of blood off her hand. "We need to talk to a wildlife vet and get some answers." That became the next plan. The three hurried back to the barn, into Bethann's office, and tore through the phone books. No wildlife vet anywhere. They called information, no help there either. "We'll have to go online. Let's all three look tonight." Agreed.

"But let's not duplicate each other's efforts," Becky suggested, sensibly.

"Okay, so how will we split it up?" Yolanda reached for a piece of scratch paper. "Alphabetically by state?"

"By state?" Mindy frowned. "What, are we going to comb the whole country?"

The three laughed, then sobered, remembering the seriousness of the situation. "Let's stick to Ohio and Pennsylvania. If they don't know what to do, with all the deer we have around here, no one will."

"Yeah, but do we want someone close by to know? What if it's something contagious and they swarm the area."

"For what?" Mrs. Butchling asked, entering the office and frowning instantly. "What are you girls up to now?"

"Nothing," Mindy said, her expression flashing from worry to innocence. "We were just talking, that's all." The three filed out past the woman, and kept going until they were outside. Close call. The last thing they needed was for Mrs. Butchling to get even more suspicious.

"She'd probably shoot the deer herself," Becky said, all three nodding. Mrs. Butchling was solely responsible for that little barn kitty being put to sleep last March. "The Bitch!"

Mindy sighed. For now, at least they had a plan. The three headed toward the barn, only to stop cold in their tracks at the sight played out ahead. The deer - the entire herd, Pixie Dust included, were loitering outside the barn door.

"Oh no."

Mindy glanced over her shoulder. Mrs. Butchling would be out in a minute or two. Even if she had to go to the ladies room, how long could that take? "We gotta get them outta here!" The three girls started toward them, arms out and talking softly. "Go, deer! Go!"

The deer just looked at them.

"Go!" The girls waved their arms, fanned out. "Go!" The entire herd just stood there. "Please…come on now, go!"

The girls started jogging toward them, the situation calling for firmer scare tactics. "Be careful with Pixie Dust!" Mindy urged. "Go! Come on, deer…go!" The deer turned, looked as if they were going to retreat, but then one and then another turned back around and trotted in their direction. It was a stampede in slow motion. The rest followed, all trotting now, coming right at them, and the girls froze! One by one the deer trotted past them, between them, around them - even little Pixie Dust, limping, but with her tail swish swishing and looking happy as can be. "Oh no," Mindy thought. They were headed right toward the arena. And sure enough, just as the thought crossed her mind, out came Mrs. Butchling.

Mindy started shouting, "Shoo! Shoo!" Becky and Yolanda followed suit. "Shoo! Shoo! Go!" The three girls ran after the deer, waving their arms and shouting. "Shoo! Get! Shoo!"

"Malaki hates deer!" Mindy yelled to Mrs. Butchling, who stood mesmerized just outside the door. "We're going to chase them away so they won't come back! Shoo!" The trio disappeared down over the hill, running like fools until they were out of sight, and stood holding their sides and laughing. The deer had gone into the woods and were now camouflaged and safe.

"I hope we didn't scare them."

"I don't know, maybe we should."

Mindy agreed. Obviously they were going to have to scare them all away at some point. "But not until we heal Pixie Dust."

As planned, that evening the girls all went online to try to come up with some information. First thing Mindy found on the Dimster was a website about, "Becoming a wildlife vet in Africa." She wondered if there were deer in Africa. Probably not, she decided, not with all the lions and tigers and bears, oh my. After all, wasn't that why some people claimed there were so many deer in the Americas; the shortage of all those lions, tigers, and bears in the wild. Why is it, she wondered, that the "eco-balance" had to rely so heavily on one thing preying on another? She shuddered. Next site became a blur as she read through it quickly. How to know if a wild animal needs help? Leave it alone, walk away....

Stand up, sit down, fight, fight, fight. She sat back and sighed, as snippets of several football game cheers ran through her mind. Push 'em back, push 'em back, wayyyy back. At dinner, she announced she was never eating meat again. Bethann gazed at her from across the table. "Good. Eat your soup. It's potato and broccoli."

~ 9 ~

Back when Malaki was first diagnosed with Navicular syndrome, Mindy thought it was a death sentence. She knew what Navicular was, she'd seen pictures of horses with it, and she had actually witnessed a horse suffering from the advanced stages. The horse could barely walk, and was old - who knew how old. It was not a pretty sight, the way it hobbled along. It broke her heart.

Mindy had scanned every book the library had on horses, and when the word "Navicular" jumped out at her, she poured over the page. "Listen to this," she'd say to her mom, who would always look up from what she was doing and nod.

Mindy was not to be ignored. From the day she was born, this youngest child of hers had something to say. She had huge, persistent lungs, so to speak. "It says here, that horses can live healthy for years and years with Navicular syndrome. It's when they actually have Navicular disease that it becomes really serious." Mindy thought about that old horse, wondered what form it was suffering from, syndrome or disease? It was probably the disease, she decided - not that Navicular syndrome wasn't serious in its own right according to this article. Early on, Bethann and Mindy decided to go against traditional wisdom, medication, corrective shoeing, pads, etc. No meds for them, just supplements; MSM and a full spectrum vitamin regimen. They had Malaki's shoes removed, and to this day she remained barefoot - with regular trimming every six weeks. So far so good.

It was actually Malaki's Navicular syndrome that started Mindy on her researching-things-to-death path. Once, she even spent close to four hours researching how chewing gum came into being. It seemed rather important at the moment, having served a detention for a chewing-gum offense the day before. It was right about then, too, that she started using the phrase, "Now I'm no expert, but..." to which her dad would always smile.

When she first learned that her father was an alcoholic, she researched that too, and decided the description didn't fit. "See, that's the problem," her dad said. "I had myself fooled, too." He was in his 15th year of sobriety, and the best dad in the world. Mindy and Bethann adored him. So did their mom.

With dinner and dishes done, Mindy sat down at the Dimster again and continued searching. "Wild-Game Wardens." *Warden,* the word had such a negative connotation. It brought to mind prisons, guards. She cringed. The first listing was about wildlife food recipes. She couldn't click off that one fast enough! Next on the list was, "Ideal places to hunt." No way. She punched in plain old "wildlife" and a science page about weather popped up. A tornado. "Hmph."

Next. "Everything about deer on eBay." Mindy chuckled. "Yeah, right." There were a grand total of 20,857 items listed. She sighed, recalling the time she and Yolanda found the perfect gift for Yolanda's mother on eBay, but then.... "No sidetracks," she told herself. She logged into another search engine and typed in, "How to treat a deer with a hoof problem?" When curious, she thought, ask exactly what you need to know. She stared wide-eyed. "A deer vet". Now why didn't I think of that? She clicked on the website and scanned the page. The vet was from Australia, the land of "down under."

"G'day!" she said out loud.

"What?" Bethann called from the living room.

"Nothing," Mindy willed the Dimster to download faster, since the information coming into view was painstakingly slow for some reason: letter-by-letter, line-by-line, inch-by-inch, and dim, dim, dim. Oh no, she thought, when the gist of the article manifested. "Raising deer for meat." She was just about to zap the site into oblivion, when a sentence caught her eye. "The average life span of a Whitetail Deer is ten to twelve years in the wild."

"Well then, my little Pixie Dust," she said. "We have to get you healthy. You're going to need those feet for a long time."

Bethann appeared in the doorway. "Homework?"

Mindy rolled her eyes to fake displeasure, exhaustion, boredom. "I'm almost done."

"Do you need help?"

"No," Mindy replied stoically, and just so as to head her off. "Did you know that a congressman gets his full pay even after he retires and until the day he dies?"

"His wife, too," Benjamin added, appearing at Bethann's side. "What are you doing?"

"Homework," Mindy said, trying ever so discreetly to get out of the page, click, click, and ultimately resorting to Ctrl, Alt, Delete. Ctrl, Alt, Delete. One more time. Ctrl, Alt, Delete. Damn Dimster! "And did you know they don't have to pay Social Security either and get that until they die?"

"Not true," Benjamin said. "They actually may have paid into it on their way to Congress, but then…." He stepped into the room and looked over Mindy's shoulder as the computer screen went blank. "What happened?"

Mindy shrugged, heaving an internal sigh of relief. "I don't know."

He nudged her aside. "What were you working on? I'll try and get it back."

"No, I'm done. That's okay."

"Has this happened before?"

"No, but never mind. What were you uh, about to say? You know, just now, about the congressmen and Social Security?"

Benjamin glanced at her, wrestling with whether to answer her question - he loved a good debate, or tackle the Dimster and the blank screen, another of his passions. "Well, it's just that…now granted, I am not saying it's right or wrong, but. A lot of the Congressmen pay into Social Security along the way, former jobs, you know like bus tables at Daddy's country club to put themselves through grad school or something similar to build strong character."

The three of them laughed.

"So, it's not like they didn't pay into it. And when you look at it that way, they could cry wrongdoing, since they actually don't get Social Security benefits once they retire. On the other hand, they obviously don't need it! Yes, they get the same rate of pay till the day they die. And on the average, even when they are working, which amounts to about three days a week, they are grossly overpaid."

"That sucks," Mindy said.

Bethann, the surrogate mom, frowned.

"Well, it's true," Mindy insisted.

"Yes, but it's accepted practice. So, unless you're going to do something about it, there's no sense complaining." Benjamin was a doer by nature.

"What do you suggest?" Mindy asked, happy to have diverted him.

"Write your Congressman."

The three of them laughed again. "Okay, I'll do that. 'Cause I'm sure they'll listen. And their wives too."

"Either way, it makes more sense than just studying the facts. Facts are only one aspect."

"Studying it?" Mindy rolled her eyes. "Oh, you know me, I'm not studying. I'm just putting my time in."

"Ah, time." Benjamin's face lit up. Time was another of his passions. He supported the theory that time is "irrelevant." Today, tomorrow, yesterday, now. "Time is the single most misunderstood aspect of our lives."

~ 10 ~

Mindy found herself sitting in the principal's office again. Her offense this time - refusing to dissect a worm in biology class. Mr. Hengesbach peered over his glasses at her and scowled. These two had a history. A good history, if obeying the rules weren't an issue. Mr. Hengesbach liked Mindy, and for the most part, Mindy liked him. He had one of those smiling faces and looked happy even when he wasn't smiling, like now.

"Okay, Mindy," he said. "You tell me. How can I let you disobey the rules, and not everyone else who happens to disagree with each and every rule we lay out?"

Mindy thought for a second. That this could possibly have been a rhetorical question never entered her mind. "Well, for one thing, I'd say there shouldn't be a rule such as this. I mean, come on, every biology teacher on earth has to know what the inside of a worm looks like by now. What do they need with my lab report?"

Mr. Hengesbach hid a smile, or so he thought. It was dancing all over his face. "It's part of the class. It's part of the curriculum."

"Yeah, well I think it's sad. I think it's sad I even have to take biology. I think it's sad to have to sit by and watch frogs being gutted." (She'd refused to do hers - that was earlier in the year.) "I think it's sad that frogs and worms all over the world die for no reason. I mean, if you dissect one and take a picture, shouldn't the rest all look relatively the same."

Mr. Hengesbach tried hiding another smile. This girl and her use of words like "relatively." He golfed with Mindy's dad, a lawyer. She was definitely a "chip off the old block."

"What do you want to be when you grow up, Mindy?" he asked, changing the subject somewhat.

"I don't know," she said, honestly. "I've thought of becoming a veterinarian, but I don't think I could handle vet school, the cadaver part, I mean. I guess I'll probably end up being a trainer like Bethann."

Mr. Hengesbach sat back, nodding. Now Bethann - there was a good student, never any trouble. At the same age, the two could pass for twins, except for the devilish look in this ones eyes. "So, is there any chance you'll go back to class and dissect the worm to avoid detention?"

Mindy shook her head.

"I didn't think so." Mr. Hengesbach heaved a heavy sigh. "It's three days this time, Mindy, starting tomorrow. I'll send your parents a letter."

"Three? Why three?"

"This is your third offense."

"No, it's not. You waived the second."

"Yes, but it still counts."

Mindy sat, pouting. "I want my worm then. Is that allowed?"

Mr. Hengesbach tried not smiling again. "Because...?"

"I want to bury it."

"I see."

"It didn't deserve to die. The least I can do is give it a decent burial."

Mr. Hengesbach agreed. "But let's not make a public announcement of this, okay?"

"Okay."

The worm's burial at Maple Dale was short and sweet. The three girls came up over the hill, shovel, Bible, and tissue in hand. May the little worm rest in peace.

"What are you girls up to now?"

"Nothing," they replied, filing past Mrs. Butchling one by one.

"Oh yeah? Well, your deer were here again."

"What deer?"

"Don't give me that. You know what deer I'm talking about."

Mindy started sweating. It was one thing to politely ignore Mrs. Butchling; quite another to be rude or disrespectful. Bethann would have a fit. Mrs. Butchling was an adult, not to mention a paying boarder. "I'm sorry. But we have to get ready for our lesson right now. Excuse us."

The three girls formed a triangle of nerves and questions in the tack room. "It's okay, it's okay," Mindy kept saying. "We'll figure this out. We have the technology."

"I say we sneak over to her house and flatten her tires," Becky suggested.

They all chuckled.

"We'll just have to come feed them later when she's not here."

"When? I have to baby-sit, and you have detention."

"Besides, I don't think deer come out at night."

"No, I think that's when they do come out."

"Then why are ours here during the day?"

Mindy shrugged. "I don't know. They're just different, I guess." All they needed was a few more days of treating little Pixie Dust. Surely the deer would move on after that. "We'll have to come after dark."

"I don't like it here at night."

"It'll be fine. We'll ask Leah Oliver to watch over us."

"Oh my God. Don't say that."

"Paleeze!"

~ 11 ~

Today's lesson was on the flat, and focused on "effective equitation." Mindy had the best seat of the three, Yolanda the best legs, and Becky the best hands. Bethann encouraged them all to be a "melting pot." Often she'd have two of them come into the center and observe, which was a bit of a challenge for Mindy. Malaki didn't particularly like another horse standing next to her, unless it was Patience, her pasture buddy. And even then, the two of them would "have words" on occasion.

"Now watch Yolanda, watch where her legs are. Sitting trot, please." As Yolanda worked her horse at a trot, Bethann had Mindy and Becky draw an imaginary line from her shoulder, down her hip - to her ankle. Perfect form, a perfect line. "Now look harder and imagine the line continuing all the way to the ground."

"What color?" Mindy asked.

Bethann laughed. "Blue. Can you see it?"

"Perfectly," the girls said.

"Good, now all three of you on the rail, spread out, and prepare to canter." Bethann waited. "And what do we do to prepare?"

"Think it, breathe it, live it," they all called out.

"Half halt, and now canter."

The deer were all but forgotten for the hour. But as soon as the lesson was over and their horses cooled out, Mindy, Becky, and Yolanda once again huddled in the tack room to plan their strategy. This time of year, it got dark around six-thirty. Often, Mrs. Butchling was there long after that. "I wish she'd get a life," Yolanda said. "I'm sure she'd be happier that way."

All three nodded like old Chinese sages.

"Okay, here's the plan. We need to do homework, and we thought it would be kind of fun to do it here, because...."

"Because...because the assignment is about...."

They blanked.

33

If the weather had been nicer and Mindy wasn't staying with Bethann, they could meet up and walk down. All three girls lived in the Maple Dale Community. As it was, they were going to need rides, particularly Mindy, since Bethann lived all the way in Burton.

"Are you sure you'll get her to bring you back?"

Mindy nodded confidently.

"Three days in a row?"

"We'll worry about that when the time comes." Meanwhile, the girls decided they should probably put out a little extra feed this evening. If they could get past Mrs. Butchling, that is. That way the deer wouldn't be tempted to come too close to the barn tomorrow.

"Maybe we could take it further into the woods," Becky suggested. Yolanda shook her head. It was already starting to get dark. "But if we hurry."

They took turns standing guard, on the lookout for Mrs. Butchling and filling their pockets in the feed room. Mindy jammed hers full of sweet feed and corn – Becky, oats, barley and more corn. Yolanda got the bran, salt, and flax seed.

It would appear this all went unnoticed.

The girls started into the woods, dark by now, but didn't get very far. The deer had gathered about two hundred feet down over the hill, and were all munching apples. "Apples?" Mindy looked up into the night. The tree overhead was an oak, not an apple tree, not to mention the time of year. And yet there were apples everywhere. "Keep walking," Mindy whispered. "We don't want to scare them."

Becky led the way, followed by Yolanda, and then Mindy. Twigs crunched and crackled under their feet.

"Whooo...."

They stopped.

"Whooo...."

"What was that?"

"I don't know. An owl?"

"Whoooo...."

"I'm outta here."

"Wait, listen."

"Whooo...."

Mindy swallowed hard and tried mimicking the sound. "Who? Whoo?"

"Whooo...."

"Let's go back." Yolanda turned.

Mindy stopped her. "Let's just go to that tree. We'll put the food by the roots."

"Whoooo...."

The three huddled together as one, taking wary steps to the tree, closer and closer, darker and darker, and there, quickly emptied their pockets.

"Whoooooo.... Whooooo...."

"Oh, shut up!" Mindy said. And in spite of it all, the three of them laughed. "It's probably just the wind." They stood still for a moment, listening, and were just about to start back up the hill, when they heard the sound of footsteps.

Crunch - crunch, crunch -crunch.

"Oh my God." Yolanda whispered.

The crunching grew louder.

Whoever it was, was walking toward them. They stared, frozen in their tracks, listening, clutching one another. "I'll bet it's Mrs. Butchling," Becky said. "I'll bet she followed us."

Mindy shook her head. "It's an animal. Listen." The footsteps had a four-beat sound to them. The girls strained to see in the dark. Along with the footsteps was the rustling of brush.

"Let's get out of here."

The three looked at one another, the whites of their eyes practically illuminated in the night, and just then, they heard a little sneezing kind of sound. Close, very close. Again, they strained to see in the dark: focus, focus, focus. There in front of them, on the trail, stood little Pixie Dust.

"Oh my God...."

The three girls stood paralyzed for a moment. Its mother had to be close by - wouldn't a momma deer be protective? Would she get mad? Would she get aggressive? Would she charge them? Would the whole herd charge them? All these thoughts ran through their minds. What if...?

Pixie Dust came closer. Crunch – crunch, crunch – crunch. Another sneeze.

"I wonder if she's got a cold?" Mindy whispered.

Crunch – crunch, crunch – crunch.

The girls stood with their backs against the tree. Mindy extended her hand. "Come here, little one. Come here, Pixie Dust."

The little deer stretched its neck, the distance in the dark disappearing as she touched Mindy's fingertips with her nose. A light touch, a nuzzling, and then a sniffing touch, sniff – sniff, and then the warmth of her tiny little tongue as she started licking Mindy's hand. "Oh my, it's the sweet feed, the molasses," Mindy whispered. "It's okay, it's okay," she said softly, when Pixie Dust frightened at the sound of her voice. "It's okay."

Yolanda reached down carefully, gathered some feed, and held it out. Pixie Dust ate it eagerly. Becky fed her some, too, and as she ate, Mindy stroked the side of her face, her neck, and then her shoulder. When Pixie Dust sneezed again, so very close, the girls all jumped. And with that, the little deer bounded away, stopping only to glance back, before disappearing into the night.

"Oh my God! Oh my God!" the girls kept saying in unison. "Oh my God!"

"Whoooo."

~ 12 ~

Malaki licked Mindy's hand over and over. She was a bloodhound of a horse, could smell food a mile away. But there was something other than the lingering scent of sweet feed that had drawn her. It was the scent of the little deer. The girls laughed at Malaki's reaction. First the casual sniff, then another sniff, then a few snorts as she backed up in her stall, turning her head one way and then the other, eyes wide, nostrils flared. Then back for another sniff, and then another, then finally to lick all the scent away and every last memory of sweet feed heaven.

"Remember that time she sniffed out the dead bunny."

They'd been grazing Legs, Andy, and Malaki on the hill, when all of a sudden Malaki started her bloodhound act, nose to the ground and edging along making sniffing noises. She looked like an oversized anteater. Then the abrupt stop, the slow-motion, wary, full-body stretch backwards, and the subsequent snorting. About ten feet away, lay a dead rabbit. With a toss of her head, Malaki deemed herself close enough. She sidestepped the rabbit, ventured another uneasy look over her shoulder, and then resumed grazing. When they told Bethann about it later, she said she'd never seen a horse do that, the sniffing. Yep, she was a tracker all right.

In conjunction with this uncharacteristic equine behavior, was her rather disgusting penchant for sniffing piles of horse manure. She'd sniff and sniff, as if she could identify the owner, and really took the job seriously. The girls couldn't help but find this habit of Malaki's entertaining. Sometimes she'd take a sniff and just walk on, sometimes she'd scan the pasture, let her eyes rest on a horse, pegging him or her. Or, she'd turn her nose up, literally, and even appeared to shudder sometimes - making no bones about liking or not liking what she just sensed. What was even funnier was when she'd walk away, and have second thoughts and have to go back and check it out again. And never, ever, ever, would she walk in it. Apparently she didn't think it was unladylike to sniff and track and sniff some more. But step in it? No way, that would be beneath her.

After Malaki grew bored with licking Mindy's hand, she set her sights on Mindy's jacket pocket, which turned into a tugging match. Mindy stepped out of reach and Malaki tried to stare her down. When that didn't accomplish anything, Malaki pulled her halter off the hook outside her stall and started twirling it round and round and round. She had the act down pat. "Feed me something, feed me something, feed me something now!" The girls laughed. They knew if they didn't walk away, she'd twirl it forever.

Yolanda's brother arrived. Yolanda left. Then Becky's mother came, honked. Becky left, then Mindy and Bethann, and hours later...Mrs. Butchling.

The girls were anxious to get back to the barn the next day. They exchanged notes whenever they passed one another in the halls at school. It was *the* topic at lunch. And it was all Becky and Yolanda talked about on the bus ride home. Mindy planned and plotted during detention. Always one to look for a silver lining, she decided having to stay after school just might work to her benefit. At least she was getting her homework done, and wouldn't have to worry about it later.

It was actually good she got it out of the way, because nothing went as planned at the barn. For some reason, Mrs. Butchling arrived late, which meant she'd probably be staying later. Or so they thought at first. And she had a black eye. Bethann fussed over her, asking what happened, if she was all right, did she need anything? But Mrs. Butchling just shook her head.

The girls were somewhat speechless. It wasn't a little black and blue; it was a major black eye. And tears kept sliding down her face. Drip, drip, drip. When Bethann suggested she might want to wear a patch over it for a few days, the girls stared, all three thinking the same thing. The patch, and if she smiled, with all her back teeth showing, she'd look just like, "Captain Hook!"

"I'll have to come back later," they heard her telling Bethann.

"That's okay. Did you want something done with Dew Drop? I can do it, save you the trip back."

"No, I'll be fine. Thank you," Mrs. Butchling said. And now both eyes were dripping.

"Do you think she's crying?" Becky whispered.

Mindy and Yolanda shook their heads. "No way. Are you kidding? She probably doesn't know how." The three of them chuckled. Then Mindy noticed something else and grew serious. "Look, she's favoring her right leg. I wonder if she fell."

Bethann talked further with the woman at her car and came back looking angry, angry at them, angry at the world. And yet sad at the same time.

Mindy apologized. Yolanda and Becky, too. "We're sorry. Did you hear what we were saying?"

"No, w-why? What did you say?"

"Nothing."

Bethann walked to the end of the barn and opened the back doors to go out and around to get a muck basket to pick out Dew Drop's stall, and there stood the deer. Four, five, six, seven of them, little Pixie Dust included. And looking so cute!

Mindy started shooing them, which took Bethann by surprise. "What are you doing? Don't scare them. Leave them alone. They'll go away. Remember, they're more f-frightened of us than we are of them."

"Oh? Okay." Mindy stood at her side, shrugging innocently at Yolanda and Becky. And sure enough, the deer turned and started down over the hill. Close call. Even little Pixie Dust scurried away. The girls went about their business then. Mindy lunged Malaki; it was not her night to ride. Yolanda and Becky groomed Legs and Andy. All three cleaned their tack. Yolanda swept the aisle way. Mindy broomed out some cobwebs in the feed room. All this, to kill time, and Bethann was still in the barn. Normally she'd be in the office by now, doing paperwork.

"Is there anything you need done?" Mindy asked.

Bethann adjusted Dew Drop's blanket. "No, thank you. Don't you have homework to do?"

Mindy started to shake her head, and caught herself. That was the excuse they used to get there. "Oh, yeah. I forgot."

"Me, too," Yolanda said. When Becky nodded as well, Bethann just looked at them.

"Life is so sad sometimes," she said. And that's all she said. The three girls filed out of the barn and into the lounge area of the arena, totally stumped as to what to do about feeding the deer. If they waited too long, Mrs. Butchling would be back.

"What if we just don't feed them tonight?" Becky asked, practically.

"What? They'll starve!" Yolanda replied.

"Shhhh."

Bethann came in and went straight to her office. Mindy thought hard and fast. "Okay, here's the plan. We're not going to be able to stay as late as our Mrs. Bitchling." The girls laughed. "So we're going to have to try and occupy Bethann for a few minutes."

Yolanda and Becky stared. "How?"

"I don't know. We'll take turns and go talk to her."

"About what?" Bethann wasn't a talker. She was nice. She was a good instructor. She was all that. But she just wasn't a talker. Besides, she seemed as if she was in a bad mood, and she was never in a bad mood. "What's there to talk about?"

"I don't know. But we're each going to have to come up with something. Who wants to go first?"

No one.

"All right, we'll flip a coin. Who's got money?"

None of them.

"Okay, we'll draw straws."

Straws they had. Yolanda was elected, and with that, Mindy and Becky snuck out the back door. Fortunately, it wasn't quite dark yet, so they could see where they were going and were in and out of the barn in a flash, pockets filled to the brim. They snuck back around and peered in the lounge window, could see Yolanda in the office, talking up a storm and waving her arms. So down over the hill they went.

When Yolanda heard them return; they were clearing their throats and making noise on purpose, she excused herself and joined them. "Okay, they're fed," Mindy said.

Yolanda let out a huge sigh of relief.

"And we put down more iodine, too."

All three opened their history books.

~ 13 ~

Bethann and Mindy's mother phoned from Kiev and caught Bethann just as she was leaving in the morning to go feed. "Hello? Hello?" Terrible connection. "Hello?"

"Hi, Mom! How are you?"

"Wonderful, dear! Wonderful? How are you and Mindy?"

"Great! Everything's fine!"

"I can't talk long. Your dad's holding a cab!"

"Okay!"

"It's really hard getting a cab here!"

"Okay!" Bethann laughed. Talking to her mom was always a trip, on any day, any given situation. "I'll pick you up at the airport!" They were due to arrive home in a few days.

"No, dear! That's why I'm calling! Your dad wants to stay another week! I told him I wasn't so sure, that...."

"Stay, Mom. Honest. Everything's...."

"Just a minute! What? Oh, your dad said we'll call you later. Just don't go to the airport, okay?"

"Okay!" Bethann laughed. "I'll talk to you then!"

"Bye, dear. We love you! Tell Mindy! Tell Benjamin!"

"Okay! Bye-bye!"

Amazing, how horses behave when you're five minutes late, Bethann thought, as she entered the barn. Oh, if they could talk, and certainly Malaki did try. Bethann smiled. Malaki was the one horse, no matter who entered the barn or what time of day or night, that always greeted them with a whinny. That high-pitched hello of hers was usually a signal that got all the other horses going. Today, she was grumbling.

Bethann went about mixing the feed and all the while, Malaki tossed her head and kicked and squealed. Patience, her stable and pasture buddy, stood in the stall next to her, waiting rather (so apropos) *patiently*. It was interesting how these two horses got along so well. It's not as if their personalities were the same. Malaki was witchy, where

Patience was kind - though Patience certainly would never stand for any of Malaki's guff. Patience was levelheaded. Malaki was prone to spooking and turning inside out at the drop of a hat.

If there were one thing Bethann could change about Malaki, it would be just that, her spookiness. It's not as if it wasn't justified, to a point, Malaki being a boss mare. Mares with that inherent self-appointed responsibility saw and heard things sooner than most horses, by nature. They were always on guard. Bethann threw in Malaki's hay and watched her tear into it. Such an appetite! Malaki pinned her ears. "You're welcome," Bethann said. "If you were in the wild, you would probably be one of the last survivors." Malaki looked keenly at her for a second and promptly went back to eating. Affirmative.

Bethann loved her job at Maple Dale. It was a dream come true. After Leah Oliver died, Maple Dale was almost destroyed, and then went through a whole slew of farm managers. Bethann was just a teenager then. In Leah's day, Bethann's position was referred to as the Headmistress. That was a long time ago. As Farm Manager, Bethann not only managed the day-to-day operations of the horse farm, she ran the whole show. She schooled the horses, she taught the lessons, she managed the staff, she scheduled the events, she took the students to the shows. She did it all.

And for the most part, it was manageable. She tried not to get involved in the lives of the boarders or her students. She tried very hard. But there were times, like last night, with Mrs. Butchling.... Don't go there, Bethann told herself, there's absolutely nothing you can do about it. She picked up the phone and called Benjamin at work.

"Uh huh," he said.

Bethann laughed. He always answered the phone that way. His mind was like a spreadsheet with a million working columns.

"Mom called. They're staying another week!"

"Okay."

Bethann laughed again. In the four years they'd been married, she had yet to hear one discouraging word out of him.

"Do you want falafel for dinner?"

"What time?"

"Eight-thirty or so."

"Ooh, too late for falafel, too spicy. No good dreams that way," he said, sounding very Asian. "Why so late?"

"Mindy's going to do homework here with her friends."

This evening was hack night, no lessons, so the girls all rode for about an hour. Mrs. Butchling was present as usual and crabby as ever, the girls observed - black eye and all. She insisted all three of them move their horses out of the way when they were back in the barn using the crossties. Normally with that many horses in crossties, a person would lead their horse up and around the back way. But not Mrs. Butchling. She did say please and thank you. Then again, she always did, though she never sounded very nice about it. Dew Drop was such a nice horse. How did he ever get such a crabby owner?

When Mrs. Butchling put Dew Drop away and headed for the office, probably to use the ladies room, (the woman peed more than anyone they knew) Mindy and Becky scrambled into the feed room to fill their pockets. Yolanda had done so well distracting Bethann last night; they talked her into taking on both Bethann *and* Mrs. Butchling should the opportunity present itself this evening. Now was the time.

"Go!" they told her. "Go! We need at least ten minutes!"

When Mindy and Becky opened the back doors, the deer were "waiting" just outside for them. "Oh wow!" Mindy should have shooed them right away, but they were so cute, all standing there and looking so expectant. And didn't Bethann say don't scare them, that they were more frightened of people than people are of them. Not so. Not with this herd. One second they were just standing there, looking like a Hallmark card, and the next, in they came.

"Oh no!" Mindy and Becky started waving their arms, trying to chase them out, but they ran past them and started to trot up and down the aisle way and run in circles. All the horses started acting up, whinnying and snorting and bucking and kicking in their stalls. The deer kept crashing into one another, which had them running around in more circles. Pixie Dust was all over its mother, head up in the air and looking like a "little pixie." Malaki starting squealing, squealing and squealing and squealing. And responding to all the commotion, in through the front door came Bethann, Mrs. Butchling, and Yolanda.

"Oh my God!" Bethann gasped.

The deer continued circling one another.

"Get!" Mrs. Butchling shouted, walking toward them. "Go on. Get!"

Mindy and Becky backed against the stall walls, and the deer started past them with little Pixie Dust zigzagging in and out of the herd. The last of the does appeared rather aggressive and in no hurry. She had one of those Malaki feed-me-looks on her face. She came right up to Becky, dipping and diving her head, as if she was going to butt her. And Becky started screaming.

"I said get now!" Mrs. Butchling grabbed a broom and started waving it to get the deer's attention. "Get!"

Pixie Dust hurried past Mindy almost to the door, but then did an about-face and came trotting back. Mindy froze. Becky froze. "Don't scare her," Mindy whispered. "Don't scare her." The brave little deer had her eyes peeled on Mindy's hand. Food. She wanted food.

Mindy reached into her pocket. She couldn't help herself. She fed her. Pixie Dust quickly ate two handfuls, and probably would have eaten more, but her mother stomped her foot and made a noise. And just as cute as can be, sneeze, sneeze, sneeze and tail swishing, the little deer trotted out of the barn and into the night.

"Did you see her?" Mindy exclaimed. "She's not limping! She's sound!"

Bethann shook her head. "Oh, Mindy."

"What?"

All three girls tried to look innocent.

~ 14 ~

Mindy and Becky sheepishly emptied their pockets into a feed bucket and handed it over to Bethann. "Don't be mad at them. This is all my fault," Mindy confessed.

"Obviously," Bethann said. "And I am not mad, I'm disappointed. I told you not to feed them and look what you've done."

"Okay, we'll stop. We won't do it anymore."

Bethann looked from one girl to the next, with Mrs. Butchling standing at her side – hands on her hips and glaring at them with her black and blue eye half-closed and the other one just plain mean.

"I knew you girls were up to something."

Bethann touched Mrs. Butchling's arm. "I'll take care of this, thank you. Thank you for your help."

As the woman walked away, Yolanda attempted to explain. "If it weren't for Pixie Dust limping…."

Bethann looked at her. "Wait a minute. You're involved in this too?"

"Uh."

Bethann drew a breath and sighed. "I take it Pixie Dust is the little one?"

All three nodded.

"How long has this been going on?"

"Weeks," Mrs. Butchling muttered, from inside Dew Drop's stall.

Bethann glanced in her direction and took another deep breath. She knew someone had been taking some of the feed, but honestly thought it was Mrs. Butchling. Good thing she hadn't approached her about it, on top of everything else.

"Well, apparently they are growing dependent on you."

"Actually, it's only been a little over a week, so…" Mindy said.

Bethann held up her hand. She wasn't listening. Something else had just caught her attention, a dull thumping noise at the back of the barn. She motioned for the girls to stay put, and walked down to take a look. The closer she got the more positive she became about the source of the noise. So much so, she only cracked the door to see.

Sure enough, it was the deer, all huddled outside and waiting. As soon as Bethann closed the door, the thumping resumed. She didn't need to look again, to know it was from one of the deer, obviously pawing. She latched the doors and looked at the girls. "Where have you been feeding them?"

"Down the hill."

"How far?"

"Into the woods."

"Then why are they at the barn?"

"I don't know."

"I don't know."

"We don't know."

"Okay, all right, okay." Bethann held up her hands. "Let me think. It's obvious we can't feed them outside the barn, or they'll never leave."

"That one momma looks really hungry," Becky said, and no sooner said, than the pawing grew louder.

"I wonder when rutting season is?" Bethann asked.

"Fall, I think," Mindy said. "Why?"

Bethann shook her head and rubbed her face. "I don't know. Obviously I can't be sure, but that hungry one looked pregnant. Never mind, that's neither here nor there. What we need to concentrate on right now, this very m-minute...." They all stared at the back door. "Is how to feed them tonight?"

"Call a game warden," Mrs. Butchling suggested, from the stall.

"No!" Mindy cried. "They'll come shoot them!"

"No, they won't!"

"Yes, they will. They're shooting them in Solon! I saw it on the news!"

Silence...but for the sound of pounding deer hoofs and the door rattling. Even the horses were quiet, listening - all ears.

"We need to lead them away from here," Bethann said, heading for the bucket of feed and the front door. "Come on, let's go." The three girls followed and when Bethann glanced back, Mrs. Butchling was right behind them and grabbing the broom again, just in case.

"Go get my flashlight," Bethann told Mindy. It was almost dark. "Hurry. We're going to go around behind the arena. Catch up with us. Once we dump the food, we'll chase them in that direction."

It sounded like a fairly good plan to all of them, but they had no sooner started around the corner of the arena with Mindy running to catch up to them, when first one and then another deer appeared, and then another...all traversing the trees and shrubs to get to them.

"Dump the food," Mindy said, out of breath and holding her side. "They know you have it."

Bethann emptied the bucket on the ground, and went to step back and tripped. Yolanda and Becky caught her from falling. The deer advanced. Mrs. Butchling stepped in front of Bethann with her broom, holding it out and actually squinting like a pirate, and Mindy couldn't help herself. She started laughing.

"They're not going to hurt us. They're just hungry."

Pixie Dust and one of the other youngsters got to the food first, and had their mouths full and chomping by the time the others found their way. They all pushed and shoved and scrambled to get what they could.

"There's not enough," Bethann said. "Go get more."

Mindy took off running, with Yolanda and Becky right behind her. "Oh my God, oh my God," they kept saying. Malaki whinnied at them as they scrambled into the barn.

"Hurry!"

They filled the bucket quickly, and ran back around the arena. The deer had almost finished eating what was there. Bethann took the bucket, dumped half, and then grabbing the flashlight from Mindy, started down over the hill into the woods. Mindy, Yolanda and Becky followed, with Mrs. Butchling right on their heels – guarding them with her life.

Mindy caught up with Bethann. "Where are you going to put it?"

"I don't know. Far away."

About a hundred yards into the woods, they came upon more apples on the ground, and kept on going - another hundred yards or so, another bunch of apples. Bethann led them further, down over the steepest part of the hill and then up over the next hill.

"Follow the yellow brick road," Mindy said, all munchkin like, marching behind her.

Bethann chuckled.

"I do believe in spooks, I do believe in spooks. I do, I do, I do believe in spooks."

The girls laughed, and started making deep-voiced marching noises.

"Ho, ya, ho…ho…. Ho, ya, ho, hooooo."

They all formed a line.

"Ho, ya, ho…ho…. Ho, ya, ho, hoooooo…"

"Auntie Em! Auntie Em!" Mindy said.

"I'll get you, my pretty!" Mrs. Butchling cried out, broom in hand.

They all laughed even harder.

"And your little dog, too!"

They'd gone deep into the woods by then and when Bethann stopped, they were all still laughing. "Okay, I think this is far enough." She dumped the rest of the food, and knowing the trails by heart, led them to the nearest one. Feeling rather satisfied, they all walked back to the barn.

"Ho, ya, ho…hoooo…. Ho, ya, ho…hoooo…."

~ 15 ~

During the ride home, Mindy told Bethann the whole "deer" story, start to finish. Bethann just listened. From experience, she knew all too well not to interrupt. Interruptions would only give Mindy an opportunity to conveniently forget pertinent details.

"And this is the only herd you're feeding?"

Mindy nodded.

That didn't make any sense, not with the amount of feed missing. "Where have you been getting all the apples?"

"What apples? You mean the apples in the woods?"

Bethann looked at her.

"I don't know. We didn't put them there."

Bethann narrowed her gaze.

"Honest. Cross my heart and hope to die."

Benjamin had the stereo blaring; they could hear it all the way out in the driveway. Bethann and Mindy laughed. They could see him dancing in the living room with his favorite pillow, held out like a queen. He'd probably just gotten home and, as was his custom, first thing, off came his shoes and socks and then this dancing. "I wonder if he'd be any different if he'd been born in this country."

Sometimes he'd go from this waltz-type of dance right into an Asian version of some kind of funky rap, ducking and diving, Kung Fu-ing and tossing the pillow all around. Or when he'd listen to Abba, and….

Mindy shook her head. "He's hysterical."

"I know," Bethann said, and just sat there.

Mindy looked at her. "Are you going to call Mom?"

"No."

Mindy heaved a sigh of relief.

"It's not as if it's an emergency," Bethann said, and laughed again. Benjamin was motioning for her to come inside and dance with him.

He'd had a "whiz-bang" day, one of his pet expressions, and told them all about it at dinner, which turned out to be pesto pasta, warm blue-corn tortillas with Bethann's homemade salsa, and salad. Mindy saved her appetite for dessert; baked apples with cinnamon and brown sugar and rice cream. She didn't really mind all this healthy cooking stuff, but in her opinion, the desserts were the best. She would never tell Bethann, but she was missing their mom's very buttery mashed potatoes and somewhat greasy gravy.

When Benjamin paused, sat back and asked about their day, Mindy glanced at Bethann and helped herself to another baked apple. The apples were McIntosh, picked last fall from a tree in Bethann and Benjamin's back yard. Bethann was happy as a clam harvesting food from her garden or plucking something from a tree. She and Benjamin planned to have an organic quinoa farm some day. It's pronounced "keen-wa" she'd say, to anyone that asked or pronounced it incorrectly, and would rattle off all its health benefits. "It was a staple of the ancient Incas and means 'the mother grain.' It's an excellent source of iron and phosphorous, and is high in fiber and riboflavin, too."

"Does it taste good?" her father had asked, in that totally supportive yet skeptical way of his.

"Yes."

Mindy liked it, though not at first. It grew on her. It reminded her of her mother's tapioca pudding, had almost the same feel. Ahhh, her mother's tapioca pudding. As Bethann recounted the day's events to Benjamin, Mindy's mind wandered further and further. She could see her mom stirring the pudding in their kitchen at home. Mindy and her dad and Bethann were sitting at the table. Bethann had originally wanted to try to grow flaxseed. But when researching it, found the climate wasn't the best in the States. Most of the flaxseed sold in this country came from Canada. There went her vision of meditating and picking every little seed by hand.

Mindy could still see their father's amused reaction when Bethann told him that. "My little flower child," he said.

"But you and mom need to make sure you're getting your omegas."

"Omegas? What about our alphas and our betas?"

Bethann laughed. "Come on, Dad, I'm serious." Bethann had gathered all the health information about flaxseed she could get her hands on; research ran in the family. "Flax has anti-inflammatory benefits for Mom's arthritis."

Her mother frowned. "Don't remind me."

"It helps protect against heart disease and cancer and diabetes and stroke. It's high in fiber...." She placed a lone flaxseed in the palm of his hand.

Her dad stared at it. "Okay, and I'm supposed to do what, just chew it?"

"No, you mill it. You grind it up. Or, I suppose you could just chew it."

Her dad popped the flaxseed into his mouth. "Oh, no…I've lost it," he said, working his tongue all around.

"Dad, come on!" Bethann laughed. She'd also brought them flaxseed oil to try. Her dad took a taste and made a face. Mindy refused to even consider it.

"You can use the milled seed on cereal, in salads and other dishes. And the oil…."

Her dad read the back of the bottle. Flaxseed oil is rich in alpha- linolenic acid that is a precursor to the form of omega-3 found in the fish oils. "Oh, well now…" he said. "I think you may be onto something here." Since no one could eat fish in Mindy's presence, in peace, it was good knowing they could get their "daily requirement of omegas" elsewhere. Even Benjamin, a primary fish eater, abstained when Mindy was around.

"I hate fishing! I think it's cruel, cruel, cruel!" Mindy had exclaimed, the previous year, just as they all sat down to a dinner of baked red snapper. "I can't eat this! Don't you know how they catch fish? They hook them!" she cried, hands held ghastly away from her plate as if it were poison. "They hook the poor little things in their cheeks." she demonstrated. "And then they pull the hook out, which probably hurts even worse, and then they let them flop around and gasp for breath. My God!"

"Mindy!"

She turned to her mother. Her mother had that look. "Don't eat the fish then. Okay? But don't ruin it for everybody else either."

Mindy stared, mouth open. "Mom, how can anyone sit in a boat and say it's relaxing and calming, when the fish at their feet are *gasping* for breath! That's just plain barbaric!"

"Some people put them in water," Benjamin had said, trying to offer a solution and wanting to dive into the red snapper, right then, while it was good and hot. "They don't let them gasp. They wait until they get them home and uh...uh...kill them humanely."

"Oh sure. And that's supposed to make it all better. Meanwhile, they've yanked them from their homes when they could have been having a perfectly nice fish day. Imagine what they're thinking in that bucket while they're waiting around to die! And what about the ones they throw back? The poor things are traumatized for life I'm sure! And what about their kids? Oh, no, there goes Daddy! Or Mommy! Oh no! Mommy, Mommy! Help, they've got Mommy!"

"Mindy! That's quite enough."

"I'm sorry, Mom." Mindy said, pushing herself away from the table that day. "But I will never eat fish again!"

The room fell silent in her wake. Everyone just sat there, looking at one another, at their plates...at the fish. "Pass the broccoli," her dad finally said, and speared a floret with his fork.

"Mindy...?"

"Yes?" She raised her eyes.

"Did you hear what Benjamin just said?"

"No." Mindy admitted to not listening. She looked at Benjamin. "What?"

"I don't think deer are supposed to have grain."

"You're kidding. Why not?"

"I don't know. I think I read once where they don't digest it properly. They're used to eating twigs and bark and stuff."

"Well that's just great. Now what are we going to do?" She looked at Bethann.

Bethann hesitated. To remind Mindy she shouldn't have been feeding them in the first place was moot at this point. Knowing her little sister, like nobody else, she hoped to guide her to a reasonable answer, at least for this evening. Otherwise, Mindy would be up all night. "Let's worry about it tomorrow. The deer seemed fine, so apparently no damage has been done yet."

Mindy nodded, placated for the moment, a brief moment. "But we can't go cut down a tree. How are we supposed to get them twigs?"

"Mindy, we're not. We want them moving on, remember?"

"Right."

"And if I catch you outside with a pair of nippers near any of my trees, you're in big trouble. Understand?"

Mindy laughed.

"Besides, you've accomplished what you set out to do and that's to get little Pixie Dust sound, so...."

"Yeah, but did you hear her sneezing?"

"Mindy, don't go there. All right?"

Mindy nodded reluctantly. "All right."

~ 16 ~

After spending hours on the Dimster researching Benjamin's claim, Mindy lay awake half the night. He was right. Deer do eat twigs. It's pretty much their main diet in the winter. Twigs, twigs, and more twigs. Mindy read all about their stomachs, which are called rumen, and about the types of trees they prefer. The problem with feeding deer livestock feed is that they depend on certain types of bacteria and microorganisms in their rumen to break down the food they eat. If they were to suddenly start eating something different, like oats and sweet feed with molasses, and flax seed and bran, they would need different bacteria to help them digest it. If they don't have the necessary bacteria, they get "acidosis." An upset stomach.

She'd half-joked with Bethann at dinner about cutting down a tree, but according to one site, that's exactly what they needed to be doing. They were supposed to lay the branches in a designated area, along the deer's network of trails, and go back every couple of days to replenish the supply and to make sure they keep turning the branches so that all the food is accessible. The amount of branches, is determined by how many deer are being fed, and monitoring the supply. If there is food put out, but not enough, it could cause fights within the herd.

"We're talking big branches here," she'd said to Bethann, who at the time was looking over her shoulder. Otherwise, the one article said, the very deer you are concerned about, the weakest, the youngest, and the elderly, will be pushed aside.

"Oh no...."

Rolled or milled oats, it went on to say, are the most easily digested of cereal grains, and would in all likelihood, cause the deer the least amount of rumen distress. It also suggested introducing oats early in the winter, so that their microorganisms could adjust.

Mindy sighed. They were batting a thousand.

They could be fed deer pellets, which are sold at feed stores. They could be fed hay or alfalfa, but again, it had to be introduced slowly, so as not to cause an imbalance in the stomachs. Feeding them apples was okay but not recommended. Such a practice was compared to feeding candy to a baby. And also, no vegetables - both were healthy in their own right, but had very little value in providing the deer with a well-balanced and nutritious diet.

"Who'd have ever guessed?"

No wonder Mindy couldn't sleep. She pulled her covers up under her chin and stared at the ceiling. Another article had said that in the wild, when food runs out, deer naturally move on. It's their nature.

"I really messed up, didn't I?" Mindy said, when reading at that point.

Bethann smiled sadly. "You didn't do it on purpose."

One article in particular emphasized that late winter was hardest on the fawns and yearlings and the old, because this population of the herd has the least amount of fat reserve. The author claimed that sometimes, they just "lay down and die." It also talked about how deer get stressed out. Humans are the biggest stress factors. Mindy thought it would have been the weather.

And dogs. The next sentence was even more disturbing. It stated that the longer deer are fed, particularly in the same area, the more concentrated the scent - the more they will attract dogs, even normally kind, non-aggressive dogs, and....

Mindy zapped the site into oblivion.

Next one said pretty much the same thing; only this one cited deep snow as a deer's biggest health threat in winter. Deep snow not only covers the grasses, leaves and low shrubs, it restricts their ability to move about. "Well, at least we don't have to worry about that." Winter was almost over.

"Yes, but it could explain why they are in the shape they're in now." It had been an extremely snowy winter, even by Lake Erie's Snow Belt standards, definitely one of "persistent deep snow," up until the last week or so. Bethann motioned for her to go the next site. They were both weary at this stage. The Dimster was wearing them down and she wanted to end the night on a good note.

This article started out with "Why feed the deer?" which sounded pretty positive at first. The main reason for feeding deer, it stated, is to prevent a large majority from die-off due to starvation. Also, if the deer survive the winter in good condition, they give birth to healthy offspring with an increased rate of survival.

"Works for me," Mindy said.

However, the more deer that survive, it went on to say, the more of a nuisance they become. They damage expensive landscaping, they become a hazard to local traffic, they contract disease, they become....

"Yeah, yeah, yeah." Mindy zapped that one, too.

"It's all true, Mindy," Bethann said.

Mindy shrugged. One more. The final site for the night, pretty much posed the same "Why feed the deer?" question, but with a twist. A potential deer feeder should do some soul searching and ask, "What am I getting out of this?" And if any part of the answer includes, "I like seeing them outside my window," then you are feeding them for the wrong reason. "If you were to feed them and never see them, would you still feed them?"

Mindy shut the computer down. "That's like that riddle, 'If a tree falls in the forest and no one's there to hear it, does it still make a sound?'"

"That's not a riddle, that's an age-old question."

"Same difference."

Bethann chuckled. It was well past midnight at this stage and they were getting a little slaphappy. Time for bed.

The two revived the conversation at the breakfast table. "Well, I've given it a lot of thought, and yes, I think I would," Mindy declared, wolfing down her toast. "Of course I'd still have to have seen them in the first place, to know they needed to be fed." She slurped her juice. "But then I wouldn't have to see them again, I don't think. Unless it was to be sure they were eating, and to see if any were being left out."

Bethann had come to some decisions of her own. "I'll stop and get some deer pellets and we'll mix it with the oats. That way I think their stomachs will be okay. And then I think what we'll do is feed them for another week or two, but take the food further and further into the woods each time. That way they'll be fed, but moving on."

"What about Pixie Dust sneezing?"

Bethann shrugged. "I didn't say it was a perfect plan." She'd been up and down all night as well. "Come on, you're going to be late." When they stepped outside, it was snowing. Benjamin told her earlier that morning before he left for work that eight to twelve inches were expected by that evening. She thought he was kidding, but to look at the rate it was snowing now, that prediction could become a reality.

Mindy was definitely going to be late for school; the roads were a sheet of ice. Bethann couldn't get up past 25 mph without the car slipping and sliding. "This is great," she said, white-knuckling the steering wheel. "Just great. Mom is g-going to be so pleased. You've got d-detentions, you're tardy...."

Mindy laughed. "How about we add *absent* to the list?"

"No way. I'll get you there if I have to carry you on my back."

The ride to school took forever. As they passed a gas station in Newbury, Mindy thought she saw Mrs. Butchling, but it wasn't her. It was a guy in a car just like hers.

"What happened to her eye anyway? Mrs. Butchling's."

"I don't know," Bethann said. But she was lying. Mindy could tell. Some people are good liars and some aren't. And since Bethann had so little practice lying.

"Did someone hit her?"

Bethann stared at the road. She was going so slowly now; she could hear the snow crunching under the tires. "Shhhh...you're making me nervous."

They rode the rest of the way in a blanket of silence.

~ 17 ~

By noon, the snow was four inches deep with the temperature dropping. If there was any lingering doubt in Bethann's mind as to whether or not feeding the deer was a good thing, it had all but vanished in the wind. It was not unusual to get this much snow this late in the season. Four years ago, they had a three-day Artic blizzard the first week in April after the trees had already started to bud. It caused a major setback for the maple trees that year.

The horses romped and played in the pastures, all snug and warm in their turnout rugs. There was nothing like a change in temperature to get them going. Malaki and Patience chased one another back and forth. It was best keeping the two of them separate from the rest of the horses. Add any others to the mix and Malaki would start picking fights and "talking trash."

"My Patience, your Patience, I don't like Patience, I love Patience. You looking at me?"

Bethann laughed, thinking about the first time she'd tried turning Malaki out with another horse. It was with this gelding named Sarna, who was a bully to say the least. He was a biting, kicking, sour, tank of a horse. Malaki wasn't actually Mindy's at the time. They'd gone to look at Malaki on several occasions and were undecided. She, too, was sour, unhappy. When the decision was finally made to buy her, they brought her home to Maple Dale for a trial. They were told she could be a bit aggressive with other horses, so who best to turn her out with, other than Sarna.

The fight was on! Malaki squared off and squealed. Boy, could she squeal. And strike! She struck like lightning. Squeal; strike, turn and kick, then back in his face. Squeal, strike, turn and kick, back in his face. Sarna held his ground for a minute or two, then thought better and backed off, literally licking his wounds. He was a perfect gentleman after that. The two even got to be pretty good buddies. Malaki hated to see him go. He was sold about five months later and she whinnied for him for days. All other attempts to find her a pasture buddy between the time Sarna left and Patience arrived, always ended in failure. Malaki either liked a horse or she didn't. There was no in between.

Later that afternoon, Bethann left the front barn doors partially open, as usual, drove to the feed store for deer pellets, and then picked up Mindy from detention. The horses had been back in the barn for hours, turnout rugs off, and blankets back on, the stalls done. Bethann liked fresh air in a barn. She could hear Leah Oliver insisting on it. "As long as the snow's not blowing in, leave them open a little. Close them up at night. No fresh air in the barn and you're going to have sick horses."

The snow was at least six inches deep by the time she and Mindy returned. Becky and Yolanda arrived shortly after. Mindy suggested they each tie a bag of the feed and pellet mix to their saddles and do a trail ride. There was nothing more fun than a trail ride in the snow, as long as the trails were still discernible, that is. Besides, it wasn't as if it was a blizzard. It was just a nice, steady snow.

"Come on, it'll be fun."

Bethann mentally debated the suggestion. It would certainly beat hiking in this weather. She didn't want the girls going alone, for fear they'd get lost. Not one of them had any sense of direction. She herself was between horses; she could take a school horse. Rocky was good on trail and could use the work

"Okay, let's do it," she agreed.

Donned in all their gear, they resembled a pack of lady warriors going into battle. The horses had on quarter sheets; warm-up blankets that lay over their flanks and hindquarters and covered the girl's legs. The girls had on their heavy-duty jackets, boots good below twenty degrees, helmets with waterproof covers, felt snuggies underneath, gloves guaranteed to keep their hands warm at thirty below, smiles from ear to ear....

Off they went, with Bethann and Rocky leading the way. "Stay up close," she said, and laughed at herself. These were intermediate riders, not novices. "Sorry."

It was slow going, even for horses. It was a heavy, wet snow, but a pretty snow. And as Mindy pointed out, there were branches everywhere at this level that the deer would absolutely love. "Right," Bethann said. "Snap one off and you'll be making snow angels."

The girls chuckled. She was referring to Malaki, who, when spooked could wheel on a dime. One second she could be going one-way, and in the next, a totally opposite direction. End result for the rider, airborne. She didn't do it for fun or meanness. She never ran off bucking afterwards. She didn't do it from lack of training. They worked hard at exposing her to as much diversity as possible. She did it from something inherent, maybe a heightened "flight or fight" response, and there was no amount of training on earth that could school that out of her.

She didn't like anything overhead either.

Mrs. Butchling once called her "Chicken Little" for freaking out in her stall when they started unloading hay in the loft above her. "She thinks the sky is falling," she'd said, as if Malaki were some kind of idiot. Mindy almost talked back to an adult that morning, but Bethann stepped in with her talking really soft kind of voice. Her older sister had such a way about her.

"Call it a quirk; call it what you like, but it's ingrained in her. A horse's back is most vulnerable in the wild. For all she knows, there's something up there about to pounce on her. She's on alert, and she's letting every horse around her know it."

Mindy was so proud of Bethann in moments like that. Actually, she was proud of her most of the time, like now. She looked ahead, watching Bethann pick and choose Rocky's footing. They hadn't come upon any deer tracks or obvious paths yet, so they were making their own way. The trails at Maple Dale were groomed in the spring and fall, so even though this was late winter and snowing, the paths still had some faint identity. Besides, Bethann had probably ridden every trail at least a thousand times over the years.

"Taking a horse out on trail routinely is good for them. And good for the rider," she'd say. Or was that Leah Oliver? "It's good for their minds; it's good for their soul. It reminds them they're horses." She'd even let them drink out of the creeks if they wanted and graze a little, so the equestrians could also "stop and smell the roses."

"Become one with your horse, feel and sense their pleasure, their joy in being a horse."

At a crossroads on the trail, Bethann stopped to point out a pair of cardinals. The male was so pretty, so bright red against the snow, and the female, so happy at his side. She couldn't imagine a life without Benjamin. "Everyone okay?" she asked, glancing over her shoulder.

"Yep."

"Yep."

"Yep."

A little further up the climb, they saw two wild turkeys, all hunkered down and just sitting there contentedly. The two birds hardly moved, their necks turning slightly as they watched the small parade go past. Obviously, they'd been there for some time; there wasn't a visible track around them. "Wish I had my camera," Becky whispered. The rest nodded. No one had told them to be quiet, no one told them to whisper, yet there was a reverence surrounding the girls, a magical feeling. The snowflakes were magnificent, falling – falling, landing on them, on the horses, on the trees...on the brush. No sounds of traffic, no humming electric wires, no dogs barking. Mindy pointed to an owl high in a tree just up ahead. The three girls stared up at it as they passed underneath. When they arrived at the place they'd left the feed last night, they were pleased to see it had been eaten. All around were deer tracks. For some odd reason, the tracks came and left from the north. "They must have gone the long way." Bethann said. "Okay, everyone stay mounted."

"Aye, aye," Mindy said, and they all laughed.

Bethann got down off Rocky, handed the reins to Yolanda, and emptied two of the feed sacks. "We'll take the rest a little further." That was the plan, to get the deer to go further and further each day, and then to just move on.

Bethann took the reins from Yolanda and mounted. Rocky was so sensible, so kind. He stood like a trooper, Legs and Andy, too. Even Malaki behaved herself, somewhat. She cast a few insistent looks over her shoulder at the food they were about to leave behind and balked a little when it became a reality. That was about it. It was as if the horses were also in awe, Malaki included. They continued on for another fifteen minutes or so, under even heavier snowfall, and came to a clearing.

"Same as before," Bethann said, dismounting. "Everyone stay put."

Malaki buried her face in the snow and started eating it. Perhaps she thought she could root around and find that grain down there somewhere. When she lifted her head to watch Bethann, sniff, sniff, I smell food; her nose was all covered in snow. It reminded Mindy of Shad, their black Lab, and how he used to love to root in the snow. Shad had originally been Leah Oliver's dog. When Leah died, Bethann inherited him, and her cat Phoenix, too. Mindy remembered them both well, even though she was very young at the time. Shad used to sleep next to her bed. They had bunches of pictures of him watching over her. He was such a nice dog. She remembered Bethann and her mom crying for days when he died - he was almost seventeen. Their dad buried him at Maple Dale. Phoenix lived to be almost twenty and was laid to rest at Maple Dale as well.

"All right, "Bethann said, mounting again. "We're going to go back a different way. If you guys want to trot when we get to the bluff, let me know."

Everyone perked up.

Bethann led them off the trail to take a shortcut. Crunch. Crunch.

"Ooh, twigs," Mindy said, and they all laughed.

Up a hill, down a hill, and over another stretch of brush. Crunch. Crunch. "More twigs," Yolanda said.

Malaki stopped and started sniffing again, then pawing.

"Probably old horse poop," Becky said, clicking to her. "Come on, move it."

"No, wait. Look…" Yolanda said. "It's scat."

"What?"

"Scat. Some other kind of animal poop."

They laughed. Leave it to Malaki. It was obviously fresh, too. It was still steaming. They all looked around, and not twenty feet to their right, stood a big buck. "Oh my God," Becky said.

"Stay still," Bethann cautioned.

He was huge.

"We're going to walk away slowly," Bethann said, softly. "Everyone f-follow me."

Rocky turned quietly, all but for the crunch - crunching. Legs followed, then Andy. But Malaki refused to move. "Mindy, come on," Bethann said.

"I'm trying." A squeeze, a tug, a drive with her seat, nothing. Malaki wasn't budging. "Come on," Mindy urged. "Come on, they're leaving you." And then, "Keep going," she told the rest. "Maybe when she doesn't see you…."

The deer stood firm and proud.

Oh my God, Mindy thought. I wonder if he's Pixie Dust's dad?

"Mindy...?" Bethann called insistently. "Make her listen."

"Come on, Malaki," Mindy said. She kicked her gently, and then again, firmer this time, pulling her head one-way and then the other. Another kick. "Come on." The deer made the first move. It took a step backwards. One little step, and with that, Malaki turned, snorting and snorting, and she and Mindy caught up with the others. When they got to the bluff, they all broke into a trot, laughing and talking. It was practically a blizzard at this point. But they were all warm and cozy in their gear and having a blast, even Bethann, once her heart started beating normally again. Mindy was her responsibility with their mom away, all the girls were.

"All right, walk," Bethann said, after a while. "We don't want them to start sweating."

Everyone slowed to a walk, the girls incessantly talking. "Oh my God, that was too cool," Becky said, the rest agreeing. As they started down the hill to the barn, they saw Mrs. Butchling standing outside the main door, all snow covered. "Go into the arena," she told them, motioning for them to keep on going.

"Why?" Bethann asked, obeying, but glancing back over her shoulder.

"It's the deer," she said.

Bethann dismounted right then and there, handed Yolanda Rocky's reins, and hurried to the barn. The whole herd was down at the other end of the aisle way. With the front doors having been left open for fresh air, there was nothing to keep them out. They weren't milling about, they weren't frantic, they weren't moving. They were just standing there, all quiet, content, warm....

"Where's Pixie Dust?" Bethann asked.

Mrs. Butchling motioned. She and the other yearlings were curled up in the sawdust, home sweet home. "Oh, my," Bethann said. "Now what are we going to do?"

~ **18** ~

"We need to devise a plan," Mindy declared, when they'd all gathered in the arena. "First thing, we need to get the horses' blankets from the barn." That made sense. "I'll go get them."

"Oh yeah, right," Bethann said. "If you frighten the deer, they'll charge at you."

"They didn't before."

"Yes, but the back doors were open then, and they're latched now. There's only one way out and that's through us. What if they feel trapped?"

"I know! I'll go though the hayloft and down the ladder. That way I won't even be near them." The ladder was closer to the front of the barn. "I'll get the blankets and I'll be right back."

Bethann looked at her. "All right, go."

"I'll guard the front," Mrs. Butchling said, still looking like a snowman...more, a snowwoman. She must have been standing outside the barn for an eternity, guarding, watching, wondering what to do and what not to do.

"I'll go, too," Becky said, handing Yolanda her horse's reins. The two took off running in the snow, up and around to the driveway going to the hayloft. They pulled back one of the doors, and hurried over to the hay chute that lay open from the hayloft floor into the ceiling in the aisle way of the barn. Together as one, they dropped to their bellies, and hung their heads down low. "Oh my God, look at them. They're sooo cute!"

"We'll have to be very quiet."

They both swiveled their heads to the front door. Mrs. Butchling was at her post.

"Okay, let's do it." Mindy started down the ladder first, Becky was right behind her. When they got to the barn floor, the horses started nickering. It was dinnertime. All the blankets the girls needed were up front by the crossties. They each grabbed two, slowly, quietly, very, very quietly, and tiptoed to the door. The deer seemed unphased by their presence, perfectly content with their life situation at the moment. "Oh no. Halters," Mindy whispered. "We need their halters." She handed Mrs. Butchling her two blankets, and grabbed all four halters and some lead ropes. Still, the deer just stood there. Mindy smiled, gazing at Pixie Dust lying in the sawdust, and then looked harder. She could almost see the bottom of the little deer's right hoof, the one she used to limp on. She tiptoed toward her. If she could get closer, she could really see, and....

"No," Mrs. Butchling hissed.

"I'm just going to take a peek."

"Mindy, no!"

Mindy sighed. All she wanted to do was see if Pixie Dust's foot was indeed healed. This might be her only opportunity.

"I said, no." Mrs. Butchling grabbed her by her jacket and pulled her out between the open doors, and the three hurried as best they could in the heavy snow, back to the arena. Bethann and Yolanda had the saddles off the horses; Rocky and Andy were both ground tied. Bethann had Malaki, Yolanda had Legs. He was starting to get a little concerned about things, so she was hand-walking him to calm him down. They all worked quickly, put all the horses' halters and blankets on, and then just stood there. They could just turn them loose in the arena. That is, if it weren't for Malaki. She'd have them all worked up and going in circles in a flash. She was already starting to paw and "thinking" about squealing. She had that wide-eyed look.

"Go get a bale of hay," she told Mindy and Becky. "Get two."

Off the girls went again. Mindy was tempted to go back down the chute, but as they were leaving the arena, she heard Mrs. Butchling reporting her earlier behavior, and then heard, barely heard, Bethann yelling after them, "Don't even think about it, Mindy!" So that was that. They each grabbed a bale of hay, and half carried; half dragged them to the arena. Bethann had Mindy take the one down to the far end for Malaki. Malaki followed, nibbling and tugging at it. "Spread it out or she'll be back up here looking to see what they have." Bethann spread the other bale into three piles up front, far apart, and the horses all started eating.

Now it was time to figure out what to do about the deer. The horses in the barn were getting a little restless. That was a major concern. They knew when it was dinnertime and the time was now! It also went without saying, that they couldn't feed them with the deer in the barn. Nor did they want to feed the herd of deer inside the barn. Who knew what chaos that might create? Some of the articles on the websites said deer could be aggressive at feeding times. The last thing they needed was a deer fight or deer injuries. And if the horses started getting riled, would the deer then start freaking out?

Snow-covered and perplexed, Mindy, Yolanda, Becky, Bethann, and Mrs. Butchling all stood outside the barn door, looking in. In spite of wearing all the gear in the world, they were starting to get cold. Another concern Bethann had, was the possibility that other boarders might arrive, even in this inclement weather.

"Well, I'm no expert, but like I said before, they haven't charged at us yet," Mindy insisted. "So…."

Bethann motioned for her to be quiet. "*Think, think, think,*" she told herself. "*Think!*"

"I'd really like to see her foot, you know," Mindy said.

Bethann gave her a stern look. "Oh please!" She wanted quiet and she meant it. The feed room was in the middle of the barn, much too close to the deer. It was a fifteen-minute ride to the feed store. She could go get more deer pellets and be back in half an hour.

"Wait," Mindy said. "I can crawl in through the tack room window." She was in her glory and marveled at her brilliance. Why hadn't she thought of this before?

"You can't." Bethann said. "They're locked." One thing for sure, first thing Monday morning she was going to phone a contractor and get a "man door" built into the sliding doors on the back of the barn. That way, even if they were latched on the inside, to keep from blowing in the wind, there would still be a way to get in from the outside if need be. "All right, here's the plan. Mindy, you and Becky go up in the hayloft, and when I tell you, start throwing down some hay." Thus said, she then slowly, carefully, quietly, began opening the doors a little wider. "Go on."

"What are you going to do?" Mrs. Butchling asked, as the girls scurried up the hill.

"I'm got to try and get into the feed room. I'm hoping the hay will distract them, or if nothing else slow them down should they decide to charge. I'll get some feed. Then you two open the doors all the way and I'll try and lead them out."

Mrs. Butchling reached for her trusty broom, hung just inside the door, and she and Yolanda stood ready. She nodded to Bethann. Bethann hesitated, and then off she went. "Now!" she yelled up to Mindy. And the hay bales started flying. One, two, three, four....

Bethann ran to the feed room, shut the door behind her and started mixing the feed. She filled two buckets to the brim. "Okay," she yelled to Mindy, and then to Yolanda and Mrs. Butchling, "I'm ready!"

They had to pull hard to get the doors to slide the rest of the way because of the deep snow. Mindy and Becky came back around to help. The deer were all on their feet at this point and advancing toward the hay. Bethann waited until the girls and Mrs. Butchling had the doors totally open in case the deer decided to stampede. She timed it perfectly. She made sure everybody was out of the way. She stood ready, and then it turned into a waiting game.

The deer were perfectly content to munch on the hay, even little Pixie Dust, sneeze, sneeze.

"I shouldn't have filled them so full," Bethann said, of the buckets. "I can't even shake them to make noise."

"If I hand-feed Pixie Dust, they'll all follow."

Bethann considered the possibilities. Inside the barn, the deer all looked rather small, less intimidating. The horses in their stalls towered over them. "Come on, deer," she said, trying that first. The deer just looked at her. "Come on, I've got food."

The deer already had food, apparently more to their liking.

"All right, go try it." Bethann said, to Mindy.

Mrs. Butchling was right behind her, the two looking like cartoon characters. When Mindy took a cautious step, Mrs. Butchling took a step. Mindy took another step, Mrs. Butchling took another step. "Goodies, I've got goodies," Mindy said, holding out her hand.

Little Pixie Dust jumped a bale of hay, the two other yearlings followed, and all three marched up to Mindy and started eating out of her hand. Mrs. Butchling stood poised, in the event the does got unruly. They didn't. Bethann, Yolanda, and Becky approached with the feed buckets and they all took turns hand-feeding the young ones. Their little mouths were so cute, munch-munch. They petted them. They fussed over them. As long as they were feeding them, the little deer didn't mind a thing. Mindy ran her hand down Pixie Dust's leg, and just like that, the little deer picked its foot up.

"Oh my God...." Mindy said. She'd probably never get another chance. Quickly, very quickly, she took a look, and immediately pried a wedged piece of glass out of Pixie Dust's hoof. The little deer didn't even realize what had happened; she was so intent on eating. One second her foot was up, the next down, and she never missed a beat. When Bethann started leading them toward the doorway, the older deer looked up from the hay and followed their young.

Bethann led them out and around the barn, slipping and sliding. Mrs. Butchling guarded her every step of the way. The girls got behind the deer and waved their arms gently to herd them along. When they got around to the back of the barn, Bethann dumped the feed in two piles. The deer started eating, and that was that. There were horses to be fed, horses to be brought in out of the arena. Mrs. Butchling had planned to ride, but said she was too exhausted now. Her black and blue eye didn't look as bad today, particularly when she smiled. They all stopped and examined the piece of glass Mindy showed them. From the discoloration, it had been wedged in there for some time and working its way out.

"It wasn't hoof disease after all. She didn't even need the iodine."

Bethann shook her head at her little sister and sighed.

"What?"

Bethann put two and two together and figured out now how this all progressed. "You probably saved it from getting infected. So for that, you did well. You all did." She hauled two bales of hay down the aisle and kicked them out the back door. "But, I have a feeling this is going to end worse than the raccoons. Ten times over."

~ 19 ~

Mindy had violin lessons Saturday mornings and hadn't practiced all week. It showed. Not only was she out of practice, her mind was elsewhere. She'd hoped the lesson would be cancelled due to the snow. The area had gotten a total of ten inches in the past twenty-four hours, with more in the immediate forecast. Though steady, it was a slow-moving snow band and thus far, the road crews had been able to keep up. There was snow piled everywhere.

Whenever it snowed, Mindy's violin teacher, Mrs. Raddison, talked of nothing but moving South. She hated the snow; she hated the gray, gloomy skies. She hated the cold, the wind - the sun and the moon. Mindy added that last part to her reverie.

"So why don't you move?"

"I would, if I could afford it. Would you like to have five lessons a week, so I can move sooner?"

Mindy laughed.

"All right, from the top."

Mindy got comfortable and began. The lesson today was a Mozart violin requiem which she found to be most tedious. Boring, boring, boring, she thought, and it showed, it showed, it showed. She closed her eyes, that didn't help. She opened her eyes; it was a dull room, all doilies and rugs. "Oh, I wish I were an Oscar Meyer wiener," she sang the TV ad in her head. "That is what I truly want to beeeee...."

Mrs. Raddison glanced up from the piano, watching her. If this child would only apply herself. Even now, with her heart obviously not into it, there was music happening.

"Cause if I were an Oscar Meyer wiener, every one would be in love with meeeee."

"Stop. I want you to play extemporaneously."

"Homework?"

"No. Now. Play whatever comes to mind."

Mindy hesitated. One of her favorite songs was "Run for the Roses" which was about Thoroughbreds and their being bred to run. She wasn't so sure she approved of horse racing, and had actually never been to a racetrack, but loved the song. She started to play the chorus.

"I know that song," Mrs. Raddison said. "I want something original."

"Okay." Mindy took a deep breath. "Breathe, breathe, breathe," she told herself, and began to play. "Breathing is vitally important, and not just for the winds and the horns," was one of Mrs. Raddison's favorite sayings. Breathe. Mindy let her mind wander back to yesterday, a light touch of the bow...the preparation, tacking their horses, mounting, the steady climb up the hill, the wind, and then the silence, the falling snow...the turkeys, the owl, the trees... the buck, fear...then laughter, Mrs. Butchling...her eye, the deer, happiness...contentment...beauty... nourishment...sleep....

Mrs. Raddison sat in awe.

"Safe and restful sleep, sleep...sleep...." Mindy sang in her mind.

Mrs. Raddison laughed. "Well, aside from that last little ditty."

Mindy smiled. "I needed an ending. It was the first thing that popped into my head."

Mrs. Raddison folded her music and sat back. "No endings for you, not with violin. This is only the beginning." She turned and looked out the window at the falling snow. "I should be on a beach somewhere right now."

Bethann was a little late picking Mindy up. As a rule, she was always on time. Mindy hopped in the front seat, happy to see her. "I was worried. I had you in a ditch somewhere."

Bethann chuckled. The two of them had spent most of Mindy's walking-talking lifetime, razzing their mom about being such a worrywart, and every once in a while they would catch one another behaving and sounding just like her.

"The roads are good."

"Are they still saying more snow?"

Bethann nodded. "How was your lesson?"

"Okay."

"Just okay?"

Mindy shrugged. Bethann loved listening to Mindy play the violin. It was as if she were a violin virtuoso in a previous life, reincarnated as her little sister. When she played violin, life all around them faded away. She remembered Mindy's first solo recital; it was the song "Memories" from "Cats." It brought tears to Bethann's eyes, their mom and dad's, too. It was both beautiful and sad. And when Mindy stood up afterwards to thunderous applause and did a silly kind of bow/curtsy thing, grinning, they laughed and cried tears of joy. For a moment, they'd lost Mindy to the song. She was back, our little girl, my little sister. "Bravo!" her dad shouted, giving her a thumbs-up. Another silly bow. "Bravo!"

Bethann had already been to the barn once this morning, and was happy to report there was no sign of the deer. All the hay she'd put out back was eaten, and the tracks led away. Maybe they'd gotten a full belly and moved on. It would be the perfect scenario. Mindy would be sad for a few days, but that would be it, Yolanda and Becky, too. They'd get over it.

The raccoon fiasco was a horrible mess, and she didn't want a similar situation. Some had gotten killed on the road, some fell by the wayside, courtesy of the barn cats, some holed up in the hayloft, an awful rancid urine smell permeating the entire barn. At one point, there were about twenty-three raccoons in Mindy's brood. It was ultimately decided that they had to be trapped, which was easy enough to do. But then they found out that is was illegal to transport or relocate them. Not good, not good. To this day, that part of the story had been kept from Mindy. Maybe their dad should have told Mindy the truth.

"Did you hear from Mom?"

"No. Howard called though."

"Howard?" Howard-the-nerd-cousin Lupinski. "Why?"

"I don't know. It's on the answering machine. He said something about your next tutoring session. He says to call him."

Mindy gazed out the window, quiet for a moment. "Do you ever think about Leah Oliver?"

Bethann looked at her. "Sometimes. Why?"

"I don't know, I was just thinking. If you say *you* didn't put out the apples, and I didn't put out the apples, then...."

"I doubt a ghost, any ghost, would go around collecting apples, and...."

"But didn't you tell me once, that she moved the jumps and planted baby trees?"

Bethann hesitated. "Um...b-but even so, that was back then. Someone collecting the apples would have had to store them somewhere. It's not like a ghost could go around picking them from a tree this time of year."

"Maybe she planned ahead," Mindy suggested.

The two of them laughed.

Becky and Yolanda awaited them at the barn. The girls were going to ride and afterwards clean their tack. It was their Saturday ritual. Bethann said they could order pizza for lunch if the delivery guy could get up the hill. They all brought some money to pitch in. "Do you think they'd go next door and bring us a Dairy Queen cake, too?"

The girls had fun riding. Both arenas were filled mostly with the weekend riders and their horses. They were a dedicated lot and were not going to give up Saturdays with their horses because of a *little* snow. They were going to ride, "come hell or high water," said one of the Lucy's. There were three of them. Lucy G., Lucy B., and Lucy C. Lucy G. was Mindy, Becky, and Yolanda's favorite. She was tall and thin, elegant and pretty, and she had a drop-dead gorgeous boyfriend. Lucy G. pitched in three bucks on the pizza as well and sat talking with Bethann in the office until it arrived. She and Bethann were the same age and friends since high school. The two of them always laughed and had a good time together. Lucy G. had also taken lessons from Leah Oliver.

Mindy decided to ask Lucy if she thought Leah Oliver's ghost could be supplying the apples. As she started into the office, she overheard part of Bethann and Lucy's conversation. It was about Mrs. Butchling and someone abusing her. From the sounds of it, that someone was her husband. Mindy's mouth dropped. "You're kidding," she muttered.

Bethann shook her head, said she'd tell her about it later and not to breathe a word of this to anyone. "I mean it, Mindy. Please. Mrs. Butchling would be terribly upset if word got out. Now promise me."

Mindy solemnly said, "I promise."

Lucy G. smiled at her proudly. Even if her very own sister might doubt her secret-keeping abilities, apparently Lucy G. didn't. Mindy felt part of a grown-up sisterhood pact. Poor Mrs. Butchling; how sad to think that her husband hit her. For sure, the woman aggravated and annoyed her lots of times. But she'd never been tempted to hit her, or even thought of hitting her, or anyone else or anything else for that matter. What would possess her own husband to want to hit her? No wonder she was so unhappy all the time.

The pizza guy interrupted her speculations. And surprise, he *was* able (at their request) to go next door to the Dairy Queen and pick up an ice cream cake for them. They all sat around the huge table in the barn kitchen and chowed down. "Life just doesn't get better than this," Becky said. "Pizza, ice-cream cake, pop from the vending machine. And horses! Who could ask for anything more?"

When the door opened, an Arctic gust of cold air blew in along with Lucy B. "There's a whole bunch of deer by the barn! Come see! They're not even scared."

Lucy G. was the first one out. The three girls and Bethann just sat there a moment, looking at one another. "Okay, we don't know anything about it." Bethann said.

They all agreed. Fat chance.

When they joined the others, standing about twenty feet from the deer and oohing and aahing, little Pixie Dust and her two little friends, brothers, sisters, whatever, turned and started walking toward them. Grain, they wanted grain.

"Mindy's been feeding them," Bethann confessed. "Mindy, you'd better go...."

Mindy and Becky met the deer halfway. Mindy patted Pixie Dust on the head; she promptly sneezed. The girls entered the barn, closed the doors far enough to keep the deer out, and hurried to mix the deer's pellets and feed. Then, wanting to get them behind the barn, they devised a plan. Meanwhile, the deer stood out in front of the barn, milling about; a little push here, a little shove there. Pixie Dust and the other two youngsters danced circles around the herd, oblivious to the power struggle going on.

Becky planted herself at the front door and when Mindy was about halfway down the aisle, Becky pushed the front doors open and stepped back against the wall. Mindy shook the feed, and one by one, with Pixie Dust leading the way, the deer all ventured into the barn and walked down the aisle way. A whinny from Malaki as they passed her stall had them all looking, a nicker and whinny further down got their attention as well, a few more whinnies. When Mindy opened the back doors, out the deer came, following her. She spread the feed in three piles; they all jockeyed back and forth for a moment then settled in on their meal. A perfect plan.

Bethann brought down hay. Becky and Yolanda and Lucy G. and Lucy B. helped. They hauled it to the end of the barn and tossed it out back. Then they all stood, watching the deer, and oohed and aahed some more. When Pixie Dust looked up and sneezed, it was as if it were positively the most precious thing they all had ever witnessed in their lives.

Sneeze, sneeze. Ah choo, ah choo.

"You know," Mindy said, something suddenly dawning on her. "I'm no expert, but I think she does that on purpose. She never just sneezes. It's only when she looks up or she sees us or hears us. Watch." As if on cue, when Mindy clapped her hands softly and called to her, the little deer raised her head and promptly sneezed. "See what I mean. I wonder if it's like a horse's nickering? I wonder if she's trying to talk to us?"

"I don't know."

"Probably."

"Maybe."

"It certainly is a possibility."

Bethann suggested they close the doors and leave the deer to eat in peace. When they checked on them later, the young ones were curled up in the hay and the does were content and munching all around them.

"Wow!" Lucy G. whispered. "Where's a camera?"

Bethann smiled. "We've been thinking that a lot lately."

"They look so happy."

"I know. It's such a shame."

~ 20 ~

Snow continued to fall throughout the day. The deer were gone at dinnertime, but knowing they'd be back, Bethann and the girls left more food out and battened down the hatches. It was a Winter Wonderland. All that was missing were twinkling Christmas lights.

Bethann and Benjamin were supposed to have dinner with friends at their favorite coffee house and listen to a singing poet. She feared their plans might be cancelled. Yolanda and Becky were originally going to come "hang out" with Mindy while they were gone and watch a movie or something. But with the weather, the three turned to plotting a sleepover. Becky was not allowed to miss church on Sunday mornings, so they had to put Bethann on the phone to reassure her mother she'd have her home early the next morning. Yolanda had a homework assignment that needed done, Becky and Mindy promised to help. Their mothers brought their overnight things to Maple Dale. That left just stopping at the video store.

The place was packed, most of the new releases, taken. Even the gory ones, which Bethann wouldn't let them rent anyway. They decided on "Sleepless in Seattle." They'd seen it at least twenty times, but never tired of it. T-L-I-T-D > They loved it to death.

The girls always enjoyed visiting Bethann's house. It wasn't quite grown-up and every room had a kind of cushy feel, because of all the couches. They settled in the den at the Dimster. "See," Mindy said, finding the answer she wanted. "The sneezing *can* be a way of communicating."

"Yeah, but it says it's a sound of alarm."

"Maybe that's when they grow up. Maybe Pixie Dust is just practicing at the moment."

They laughed.

Something else they found out. Whitetail Deer can run up to 40 mph. They can jump a nine-foot fence. They can broad jump up to thirty feet. And they can swim 13 mph. "Wow!" Also, their coats are reddish-brown in the summer and turn grayish-brown in the winter. The change of color helps to camouflage them. And they chew cud, like a cow. They have a four-chambered stomach and regurgitate their food.

"Yuk."

It certainly explained why and how they could eat so fast. They hardly chew their food when feeding. They just swallow it. The chewing part comes later, while resting. Stomping? They stomp to communicate. When Pixie Dust's mother stomped because the little deer was lagging behind, the precise way she stomped meant something. No wonder Pixie Dust took off after her. Probably saying, "Yes, Mom!

I'm coming!" In addition to stomping and sneezing and squealing to communicate, the girls read all about how deer leave a scent along the trails from the glands in their legs, that says volumes to other deer. A deer's nose is a hundred times more sensitive than a human's.

"Awesome!" Yolanda said.

Deer tracks are heart-shaped. The girls nodded; they knew that. The pointed end of the deer tracks shows the direction the deer was going. The girls knew that, too.

"What's Bethann making us for dinner?"

"I don't know," Mindy said. "Something good."

"Do you think she wants help?"

"No."

Deer travel in narrow paths, which are called trails. "Duh?" Becky said, another given as far as they were concerned. Trails connect usually where the deer eat and rest.

"With all the snow, that would be hard to find."

Deer sleep in what is called a "deer bed."

"Not our deer. I bet they'd sleep in a stall if we let them." Deer beds are usually surrounded by plants or shrubs and protect the deer from rain and snow. Deer beds are easy to spot in the snow. "We'll have to go look for one."

Bucks mark their territory by removing bark off the trees with their antlers. This practice is called a "back rub." Bucks do their back rubs from September to November.

"Too late."

Back rubs are usually seen one to two feet off the ground.

"Hmph."

Deer do not have upper teeth in the front of their mouths. A deer uses its back teeth to twist off twigs to eat. Similar to horses, a deer's age is determined by the length and wear of its teeth. An adult will have six incisors and two canines in the lower front, six premolars and six molars in the lower back and the same in the upper back. Females are does, males are bucks, babies are fawns. They knew that. In the winter, bucks shed their antlers.

The next paragraph started out with, "During deer hunting season...." Time to move on.

"Look up Lyme disease."

"Why?"

"I don't know. Curiosity."

Lyme disease. "Okay." The main risk factor for Lyme disease is exposure to ticks that are infected with Lyme disease. The girls shook their heads. "No kidding," Mindy said. Several factors may increase the risk. The three of them leaned closer. Working or playing in wooded areas, gardening, yard work, hiking, camping, fishing (Mindy cringed), hunting, having indoor/outdoor pets. Dogs and cats can bring them inside. They can't pass the disease to humans, but if the infected ticks drop off the animal and bites the human.... Mice. Where there are mice, there are ticks. "Wonderful." What barn didn't have mice? Ticks are most active during the warm months of the year, May through November.

"Cool, we're safe then."

The risk factor for getting Lyme disease increases the longer a tick is attached. "Ooh." If you remove the tick within thirty-six to forty-eight hours, it is unlikely you will get Lyme disease. The way to remove them is to....

"Let's not go there," Mindy said. "Our deer don't have ticks. It's too cold."

Bethann walked down the hall to check on them. "Did you call Howard?"

"Not yet. I'll do it now." Mindy dialed his number and plopped down on a chair across the room. "Hi, Howard, it's Mindy. What's up?"

"Uh...."

"Bethann said you left a message."

"I did, just a minute." He apparently put the phone down to go do something and came back. "Um...."

Yolanda and Becky looked up the word "nerd."

"She said you said it was about the tutoring."

"It was, in a way. I wanted to let you know something. I'm really not your cousin."

"I know."

Nerd - an unstylish, unattractive, or socially inept person; *especially*: one slavishly devoted to intellectual or academic pursuits <computer <u>nerds</u>>. "That's Howard," the two girls said.

"No, I mean really. I've been analyzing some data, and even if we were to uh, like marry or something, it's legal." "What?" Mindy laughed. "What are you talking about? I'm not going to marry you."

Becky and Yolanda turned and stared, then stared some more. Was that Mindy? She looked different all of a sudden. Girly.

"Okay, but just so you know."

"Okay, so I know. Big deal. Not that I'm going to take your word for it." Mindy laughed again, oblivious to Becky and Yolanda. "So, as far as the tutoring?"

"I'll be there."

Mindy nodded. "And this couldn't have waited?"

"No," Howard said, without a second's hesitation. "I wanted you to know."

"Okay. Well, I've gotta get going."

"Me, too. Bye," he said.

"Bye." Mindy hung up and just sat there for a moment. Weird, she thought. And when she finally noticed Becky and Yolanda staring at her, she felt her cheeks grow warm. She was blushing for some reason, something that struck her as even weirder than Howard.

~ 21 ~

As soon as Bethann and Benjamin left, the girls put the movie in the VCR in the living room and got comfortable. Bethann had made them a feast of finger foods with all sorts of dipping sauces. They each had a comfy couch all to themselves: blankets, pillows, hot chocolate, and plates on their laps. "When are we going to do your homework?" Becky asked Yolanda.

"Tomorrow morning. I don't even want to think about it tonight."

"What's this peanuty stuff?"

"Peanut sauce."

Becky laughed. "No wonder then. It tastes like peanuts."

"What's this?" Yolanda held up a square-cut piece of something spongy-feeling.

"Tofu."

Yolanda made a face.

"Try it," Mindy said. "It's pretty good. Dip it in the honey ketchup."

"You're kidding?"

"It's not bad. Honest."

Shhhh.... The movie was starting.

"Turn it up."

Becky had the remote. She pressed the volume button, and then pressed it again. No sound.

"Here, give it to me."

Becky tossed it to Mindy. She pressed the button. Nothing. She pressed it all the way, nothing, and got up and went over to unload and reload the video. Still nothing; a great picture but no sound. "I'll go try it in the other VCR." She took it into the den, tried it there, and came back truly bummed. "It's the video. It's bogus."

"Is there a phone number on it," Yolanda asked.

"Yeah, why?"

"I'm going to call and tell them."

"What for? Do you think they'll come bring us a new one?"

"No, but they'll know we're not happy." She dialed the phone and sat up nice and straight like a grown-up. "Hello. We were in earlier and rented a copy of 'Sleepless in Seattle.' Well, there's something wrong with it. It has no sound."

The guy apologized half-heartedly. "If you want to bring it back in, we'll exchange it."

"No, we won't be able to do that. But if you would kindly make note of it, we will be expecting a refund." The guy took the information and without another word, hung up. "Oh my,

God. That was so rude." She dialed him right back. "Hey look, buddy, you just hung up on me and that wasn't very nice. Oh yeah? Well, I don't care about the snowstorm. That was rude. Good-bye."

"Do you want to watch it without sound?"

Why not? They knew most of the words anyway, and got all the way to the part where Jonah called the radio station the second time. "She's a ho!" they all shouted. "My dad's kissing a ho!" That's when the screen went blank. No sound, and now no picture. Mindy extricated herself from her blankets and pillows, ejected the video, shook it back and forth, and then tried it again. Nothing.

Nothing, nothing, nothing.

Yolanda scanned Bethann and Benjamin's video shelf. "Yoga. Tai Chi. Qi Gong. Meditation. Nature Sights and Sounds. Persian Sun." She picked the last one. "Let's watch this." It was a home video of Bethann riding Persian Sun in a horse show. The subtitle on the video read, "High Point Trophy."

Bethann and Mindy's dad had just gotten a new video camera and had documented the entire day. "This is Bethann waking up. Wakie, wakie!" Bethann covered her face with a pillow. "This is Bethann eating a hearty breakfast. What's this, Cheerios, toast, juice? Yum, yum."

Bethann looked at her dad and rolled her eyes.

The girls chuckled.

"And this is Bethann's lovely Mom."

Their mother shook her head, smiling.

"And who's this…?" He panned the camera down to the floor, and there stood two-year old Mindy. She was holding onto Shad's collar, dog in one hand and her "blanky" in the other. "Why, it's Mindy. Hello, Mindy. Say hi to Daddy."

"Awe…look how cute you are," Becky said.

Little Mindy hugged Shad for the camera, all smiles. "This calls for a close up," her dad said. A blur filled the screen as Shad licked the lens.

"Isn't that the dog that used to be Leah Oliver's?"

Mindy nodded, smiling sadly. He was such a cool dog.

"Your mom hasn't changed a bit."

"And who's this?" their dad said. "Why, it's the infamous Phoenix the cat." Phoenix jumped onto Bethann's lap, paws on the table then, and started licking her empty cereal bowl.

"Oh, dear." Their mom removed the bowl and like magic, they were at the horse show.

"Wow!" Yolanda said. "He is so pretty!" Both Becky and Yolanda had seen pictures of Persian Sun before, but this was their first time actually seeing him "walking and talking." He was nickering, Bethann astride. Her mom was standing close by, with Mindy in her arms and Bethann was looking down at them, smiling.

"You nervous?" their dad asked.

"Just a l-little," Bethann said, glancing at him.

Mindy was reaching for her. She wanted up on the horse.

"Our first class of the day, starting any moment now, is English Pleasure. Bethann has warmed up Persian Sun sufficiently and we are ready. Right, Bethann?"

Bethann shrugged, not so sure.

"Stop! Oh my God, back it up," Yolanda said.

"Why?"

"Just back it up, look...right there."

"Where?"

"That shadow, there! Beside your mom."

Mindy and Becky didn't see a thing.

"Back it up again. See! There, there it is."

Mindy and Becky stared, no clue.

Yolanda got up and showed them. "Right here. Look. Don't you see it?"

"The glare?"

"That's not a glare, look at it. It's a ghost."

Mindy and Becky stared more intensely, collective chills running up and down their spines. "Oh my God."

If they hadn't watched that show on apparitions during this past Halloween season, they probably wouldn't have thought to look for ghosts in a photograph or on film. But now, looking at it harder and harder, again and again,

Yolanda was right. It *was* a ghost. It was the perfect shape of a person.

"Oh my God, it has to be Leah Oliver." They searched through the whole rest of the video, not once, not twice, but three times. The ghost never appeared again. But in their minds, there was no doubt. Leah Oliver was there that day, watching over Bethann and Persian Sun. "Who else could it be?"

"I can't believe no one noticed before. Don't you all watch this?"

Mindy shrugged. "Not really. She'd seen it a couple of times before, but not for years and years now. It made Bethann sad to watch it. She hadn't had a horse since, that she loved as much as Persian Sun.

"We'll have to show it to her."

Mindy hesitated. She wasn't sure that was such a good idea. What if it made her feel sadder?

"What if the ghost wasn't there before, and is only there now?"

"Can that happen?"

"I don't know." More chills ran up and down their spines. "Wow...."

The three sat in utter silence for a moment.

When the grandfather clock across the room struck the hour, they all jumped!

"Oh my God," Becky said.

They all looked at one another.

This was going to haunt them to no end. "I think we have to find out," Mindy said, in a hushed voice. "We really need to know if it was Leah."

"What do you mean? How?"

"I think we should have a séance?"

"What? You're kidding, right?" Yolanda said.

Mindy shook her head. "No, I'm serious."

Becky was all for it. "What'll we do?"

"We'll need a candle, I think." Mindy said.

"Oh, great," Yolanda said. "We'll probably burn the house down."

Mindy laughed. "Come on, it'll be fun."

Becky was up and already looking for a candle.

They'd have to hurry. It's not like Bethann and Benjamin were going to be gone all night. Mindy and Yolanda peered out the window. It was still snowing. "Grab the pillows," Mindy said, and pulled the drapes. By the time Becky returned with a candle she'd found in the den and matches from the kitchen, Mindy and Yolanda had the pillows all set in a little circle. "Sit, my fellow ghost hunters," Mindy said, with a bow. "I am your Madam Guru." They all laughed and sat cross-legged on their pillows.

Yolanda lit the candle then and blew out the match.

"Ooh, lights." Mindy got up and turned off the lights and sat back down, but it was still too bright. The lights from the kitchen and the den were creeping in. She got up and turned them off, too. "I can't see," she said, from down the hallway in pitch black.

Yolanda took the candle, found her, and showed the way. "Oh my God, I feel weird already," she said, her face illuminated.

Mindy nodded. "Me, too."

They formed a circle, holding hands, and sat quietly looking into the flickering flame.

"Are we sure we want to do this?" Yolanda asked.

"Yes, oh Doubting Flower," Mindy said, and they all laughed. "Quiet, quiet, let's get serious."

"Well, you're the one that called me Doubting Flower."

"I apologize," Mindy said, in a very, very serious tone of voice. "I apologize to you, I apologize to the gods, I apologize to the spirits."

"I don't think we should say God," Becky said. "I don't know if he approves of this type of thing."

"Okay, I'll start over."

The house creaked.

"It's the wind."

"Let's hope so."

"We are calling upon the spirits of other worlds," Mindy said.

The three girls looked at one another, the candle's flame dancing in their eyes.

"We are specifically calling upon Leah Oliver," Yolanda interjected.

Mindy and Becky looked at her.

"What? What if there's someone out there listening we don't want to talk to - like an ax murderer or something?"

Good point. Mindy and Becky nodded. Mindy cleared her throat. "We are calling upon the spirrrrit of Leah Oliver," she said, and immediately, Becky and Yolanda started laughing.

"We can't help it. It's your voice. Talk normal."

"Okay, okay." Mindy drew another deep breath. "Leah Oliver, you don't really know us, but." She looked at Becky and Yolanda. They nodded their approval. "We come to you tonight...."

Becky started laughing again. "I'm sorry."

Mindy heaved a sigh. One more time. "Leah Oliver, we are worried about our deer."

That sobered everyone, Mindy included. She couldn't laugh now even if she tried. "We are worried about their health and their well-being. And we think you're worried, too."

Becky and Yolanda nodded.

"If you are here," Mindy said, hesitating. "Could you please let us know?"

They sat and waited.

"Call her again," Yolanda suggested. "Maybe she didn't hear you."

"Leah Oliver? Leah Oliver, are you there?"

They waited some more, and then took turns voicing what was on their minds.

"We want to know if you were at Bethann's horse show."

"We want to know if you're the one that's putting out the apples."

"We want you to help us take care of the deer."

"We want to know if you are happy."

"We want to know if ghosts are real."

The house creaked again, louder this time.

"We want to know if you care."

"We want to know if are living at Maple Dale."

A huge gust of wind rattled the house. And with that, the candle flame went out.

~ 22 ~

By the time Bethann and Benjamin arrived home, every light in the house was on. The girls were still somewhat spooked, but didn't dare confess to having a séance. Bethann said the roads were really bad and that it was snowing pretty heavy. "We could see the house from all the way down the end of the block. Thank you. Good thinking." She suggested they go to bed soon, as they'd probably have to leave very early in the morning to get Becky home on time. Bethann was in a good mood as she bounced around the house turning out lights, already planning breakfast. Benjamin said he'd had too much of a good time and went on to bed. He pretended to be tipsy – the girls laughed. With him gone, Mindy was tempted to bring up the subject of Leah Oliver, but couldn't decide on a way to mention it casually. Yolanda suggested they all act like that hadn't seen the Persian Sun video already this evening and try to get Bethann to watch it with them. However, Mindy thought it might upset her. It would be bad enough watching a video of a horse she loved and still missed to this day, let alone the equivalent of, "Oh look, is that the ghost of Leah Oliver?"

"Shhhhh…she'll hear us."

"Did you guys get enough to eat?" Bethann called from the kitchen.

"Yes, thank you." They'd cleaned the kitchen spotless. The living room, too. Nervous energy.

"Tell her I need to do my homework. Tell her it's about ghosts."

"No."

"Come on, that way we can ask her."

Mindy hesitated. She really would have liked to know more, but then what if it ruined Bethann's night? After all, wasn't she being very understanding about the deer.

"Mindy, come on...."

"No, not tonight. Maybe on the way tomorrow."

Bethann entered the room with a curious expression on her face. "Why does it smell like smoke in here?"

Mindy seized the opportunity. "We weren't smoking or anything like that, if that's what you're worried about. We lit a candle."

"Why? Did the power go out?"

"No, um...." Mindy hesitated. "We had a séance."

Bethann looked from one to the next, yawned, and held up her hand. "Good night. No more. It's been a long day. Good night."

"Good night."

Every once in a while, Bethann had an occasion to act like a mom. This was one of them, and the girls responded accordingly. They all got comfortable on their respective cushy couches and very shortly were fast asleep. It was Bethann who lay awake well into the night.

She was a bit cranky in the morning, as a result, and was not pleased to find that the girls hadn't gotten Yolanda's homework assignment done. "Eat quickly," she told them, placing a stack of feather-light buckwheat pancakes in front of them. "And then go do it now. Come on, eat." Everyone had slept in. "If you don't get it done, you can finish it in the car on the way to your house."

It was an English assignment, a book report. "Too bad it wasn't history," Mindy said. "We could make something up. What's the title?"

Yolanda was in the Honors Program and read from a different list of books than the other two.

"The Education of Little Tree."

"You're kidding," Mindy said. "What luck! I read it. I loved it. Give me a pencil."

"How long ago?"

"Don't worry. You don't forget a book like that."

"Okay, so what's it about?" Yolanda asked, somewhat skeptical.

Mindy licked the tip of the pencil in preparation. "Uh...it's about a little boy who is part Native American, and something happens to his parents and he goes to live with his grandparents. They live out in the wild, and they're like two trees in the forest. That's it! That's the author's name. It's Forrest or treetop or something."

Yolanda nodded, looking at the book cover.

"And he learns all sorts of lessons from his grandparents, and there's some missionaries who want him to not act like an Indian. The two trees are about how a couple should be strong and tall, and stand on their own. But that sometimes the winds blow, and how they support one another. It was really cool."

"How does it end?"

"Well, the grandfather dies, and then the grandmother. I really liked her. She kept putting extra sugar in things and acting like she spilled it. One or the other, the grandmother or the grandfather says "I kin ya" before they die, which was really cool. It means I love you or something. And then there's this saying about meeting on the other side. It was a great book. I'm serious," Mindy said, writing and talking at the same time. "I remember wanting to strangle the missionaries. Great book!"

Fortunately, Bethann had read the book as well. She'd actually read it to Mindy early last year. She looked over the paper, corrected some mistakes, added a fact here and there, and all Yolanda had to do was copy it in her own handwriting on the way. Yolanda finished just as they were pulling into the Maple Dale Community. It was still snowing. Bethann dropped Becky off first, then Yolanda. All was well, assignment done, home on time. And then she and Mindy drove to the barn. The deer were at the back door waiting for them.

Bethann sighed. "This is not good. They're never going to leave."

"Yes, they will. But I think we're going to need help."

"What do you mean?"

"Leah Oliver."

Bethann shook her head. "Oh, Mindy. I only wish...."

"I think she's still here, or at least maybe here sometimes."

"You don't get it, do you? If she's still here, then she's still in limbo. Besides, she's not here or I would know. She's been gone for years. It's good for her to be gone, Mindy. Let it go, okay? We'll have to figure this out on our own."

"Okay."

"Now for the time being, here's the plan: you get the grain, I'll get the hay."

Mindy nodded. "Maybe once the storm passes...."

"I hope so. Otherwise, I don't see this having a happy ending."

"I'm sorry," Mindy said. "I never meant to cause you trouble."

"I know."

"When is it supposed to stop snowing?"

"Who knows? Tomorrow, Tuesday, next year. Come on, I hear Malaki."

Mindy listened and then chuckled. Yep, it was Malaki. Her whinny was one of a kind, in all its variations. This one was her "I'm about to get upset, I'm hungry, where have you been, it's about time," whinny!

The two entered the barn, after having to shove and push and bang on the front door to loosen the track, closed the door behind them, and quickly went about their business. Mindy mixed the grain and pellets for the deer, Bethann dropped down hay, hayed the horses, then walked down to help Mindy with the back doors. They were jammed shut with snowdrifts. More pushing and shoving and banging. Bethann turned around and started kicking them from behind like a horse. Mindy followed suit. The real horses could care less about all the noise. They had their hay; their grain would be materializing soon. Life was good.

Finally, they got the door to budge, just wide enough for Mindy to try and squeeze out.

"Don't even think about it," Bethann said. "What if they stomped you? What would I do then?"

"They're not going to stomp me. They just want to eat."

Bethann banged and kicked the door some more, and got it to open a little wider. Pixie Dust was standing behind her mom, the two other youngsters huddling close by their dam. They all had their backs to the wind, and for a moment, looked like snow-covered lawn ornaments.

"It's too cold," Mindy said, clearing away the snow with her foot so she could dump the feed. "They need shelter."

"They're deer, Mindy. They *live* outdoors."

Mindy dumped the feed in three piles and backed up. "They need a deer bed."

"And blankets too?"

Mindy laughed.

Pixie Dust was the first to the feed, a scout of sorts. She had a mouthful, her little tail swishing, when the rest followed. "Help me with the hay," Bethann said. Before they got the hay to the back door, little Pixie Dust had made her way inside the barn, and was eating, turned around - facing out, that cute little tail of hers swishing a hundred miles an hour. A little stomp, another little stomp.

"How could anyone shoot them?" Mindy asked.

Bethann kept her head. "They don't shoot the young, there's not enough meat."

Mindy's mouth dropped.

"I'm sorry, but Earth to Mindy...?" Bethann grabbed a bale of hay in each hand and advanced, thinking the little deer would run out when they got close. It did not. It was not phased by human presence in the least.

"Shoo her out," Bethann said.

"What? And scare her?" Mindy put the hay down and touched Pixie Dust gently on the shoulder. The little deer looked at her and sneezed, then went back to eating the grain and swishing her tail. "Well, we could try and open the doors a little more, and...."

"And what, have all of them in here? No thank you. They're wild animals, Mindy. Do you understand? *Wild animals.*"

The two other youngsters poked their heads through the doorway at that point; all snow covered and wide-eyed.

"Kings and Queens of the for-r-rest," Mindy sang, and then, voice changing, "If I only had a heart."

Bethann let go of the hay, held up both hands as if to say I give up, and walked away. "If you get yourself hurt, I'm going to kill you," she said, glancing back over her shoulder.

"Where are you going?"

"To grain the horses. And when I'm done, that little deer's out of here!"

Mindy sat down on a bale of hay and ran her gloved hand over Pixie Dust's back. The little deer shivered. Mindy slowly removed her glove and touched her again. "She's cold, Bethann," she said.

"She's a deer, Mindy."

"And such a little cutie."

Mindy could hear Bethann sigh from all the way at the end of the barn.

"How's your foot, little one?" Mindy asked.

Pixie Dust looked at her and sneezed again, spraying her with food. When Mindy laughed, the other two youngsters ducked their heads back outside. "Are you a little boy or a little girl?" Mindy leaned slightly to take a look. A little girl. "I'll bet your brave friends are boys," she whispered, laughing at her own joke. She waved to Bethann; watching her from the feed room. "We're fine. All is well."

Bethann shook her head.

The two youngsters peeked back in.

"Ollie, Ollie in free." Mindy said, softly. And to Pixie Dust then, "It's a game." She stroked her shoulder, and then her neck, her ear. Another sneeze, a little stomp. "That foot's just fine, now isn't it? Good girl."

Malaki pricked her ears when she heard her say "good girl," and when she heard her say it again, stuck her head out of her stall and nickered. "Good girl," was a phrase Mindy used often with Malaki, a reverse kind of psychology. Malaki liked the sound of it.

"Ahhhh...that's my girl," Mindy said, smiling at her. "You're the original good girl."

Malaki went back to eating.

"I'm too happy," Mindy called to Bethann.

No comment.

"If I died right now, I'd die a happy woman. Well, almost a woman."

Bethann looked at her from the feed room, and something about the look in her eyes.... "Oh my God, I'm sorry, Bethann." Oh my God, I can't believe I said that. Leah Oliver died here in this very barn. "I didn't mean that. I'm sorry."

"I know. Just play with your deer, okay?"

"Okay." Mindy glanced down the aisle way. Leah Oliver's students had found her lying on the cement. Bethann was the one who called for the ambulance. "I can be so stupid at times," Mindy told Pixie Dust, stroking her neck. "I don't mean to be, it just happens."

"Mindy, enough. Okay?"

"Okay."

~ 23 ~

The deer were there for lunch. The deer were there for dinner. With all the snow on their backs, they were starting to look like mammoths. So much snow! For the first time in West Geauga Schools' history, classes were cancelled in advance of a school day. "Stay off the roads," the news people kept insisting. "Don't go out unless it is an emergency. Don't go anywhere. Follow these guidelines in case of a power outage. Stay put. Stock wood. Don't turn on your gas cooking stoves for heat. Don't use faulty kerosene heaters. Layer, but don't overdress. Have a battery-operated radio on hand for updated reports. Don't eat uncooked meat."

"Hmmm," Mindy said, frowning. "If we can have cell-phones, why can't we have cellular electricity? Why do we have to have wires?"

"I don't know," Bethann said. "Ask Benjamin."

"I will."

The two of them were still at Maple Dale, waiting to hear from the snowplow lady. Bethann had decided they should stay at their parents' and Mindy's house in light of the increasingly bad weather. The house driveway hadn't been plowed yet, as it was on a "per-push" basis this time of year.

"I think it's so cool that Audra plows," Mindy said, looking out the window. Audra was Sydney's mom, one of the equestrian students at Maple Dale. She and her husband David both plowed, splitting their route, but as a rule Audra always did Maple Dale and any of the homes in the Maple Dale Community on their list. She said she'd get the house driveway done as soon as possible, but that since it hadn't been plowed at all in the past three days, it was going to take a while. Mindy was bored to death waiting. Truth was, she was a little homesick for her own room, her own things. "There's no place like home," she said, clicking her heels. "There's no place like home."

Bethann smiled her first smile all day. "Why don't you take a nap?"

"I tried. Apparently, I'm not sleepy."

They had all the comforts of home here at Maple Dale; kitchen, bathrooms, couches, television, heat, phone, vending machines. Maybe if Becky or Yolanda were here, it wouldn't be so bad. As it was, every minute was torture. All she could think about was the deer freezing out in the blizzard. If they had deer beds, then why weren't they in them? Why were they just standing at the back of the barn? Why, why, oh why? She agonized and agonized and came up with an idea.

"Bethann?"

"What?"

Her sister had been using this opportunity to get a head start on her billing for the month.

"Do you know that old straw we have up in the hayloft?"

"No, Mindy," Bethann said. But not as in no, I don't know what straw you're talking about. It was clearly and emphatically, no - the subject is closed. Period.

Mindy hesitated. "It's just sitting up there. There has to be at least ten or twelve bales."

"Fourteen," Bethann said.

"What if I stacked them out back to make a deer bed? They're forecasting snow all week now."

"I said no. I'm finally nice and warm, and I'm going to stay that way."

"I don't understand how can you say that when the deer are so cold?"

"They're animals, Mindy. For heaven's sake, just shut up, okay? Why do you do this? Why do you *always* do this?"

"Because," Mindy said, woefully. "I gotta be me."

Bethann looked at her and tried not to laugh. Don't, she told herself. Don't do it. You'll only encourage her. But in the end, she had to laugh. She couldn't help herself. Mindy was just too funny and these expressions of hers were priceless. "All right fine, but I'm not helping you and I mean it. If you want to freeze your butt off, go right ahead. That's entirely up to you."

"Cool." Mindy started bundling up.

"And don't you dare get sick."

"Yes, Mom."

"Don't Mom me," Bethann said, and they both laughed. They couldn't begin to count how many times they heard their mother use that expression. "Mindy, wait...."

Mindy looked back from the door.

"Throw them down and I'll come help."

"You don't have to. I can do it myself."

"I know. I'll be there in a minute."

The deer were gone, so the job was easier. Their absence bolstered Bethann's spirits. Maybe the herd had finally moved on. Maybe they were like wolves and just needed to totally fill their stomachs before relocating. She hoped so, as feeding them was getting rather costly. Good hay this time of year was scarce. The last load delivered was $5.50 a bale.

They stacked the straw three bales high in a basket weave half-octagonal pattern just to the left outside the barn's back doors, used some pieces of old plank fence rails for a roof which they secured with baling twine, then spread the extra two bales of straw for bedding and put out another bale of hay. It would all be covered with snow soon, but at least the shelter would shield them from the wind, and the straw would keep them up off the ground. That's if the deer returned, and if they decided to use it, and if....

"They'll love it," Mindy said, happy as could be. "Shelter and food: who could ask for anything more?" It looked like a manger. "I wonder if we should put out water."

"No." Bethann said. "They can eat the snow. Water would be solid ice in no time anyway. Come on. I'm chilled to the bone."

Two phone messages awaited them on the answering machine. The first one was from Audra; she'd just finished plowing the driveway at the house. "You're good to go," she said. The second was from Benjamin. His estimated time of arrival at the "in-laws" was 7:35 p.m., about fifteen minutes from now. This was going to be a first for him, staying overnight at Bethann's parents' house. He sounded a little nervous.

Mindy, hopeful, headed straight for the refrigerator freezer when they got home. "Awesome! Yes!" There sat her mom's lasagna - a whole big pan of it. "Thank you!" she cried out to any spirits available. "Thank you!"

Bethann walked through the house turning on lights, adjusted the thermostat, and put on a pot of water for tea. She couldn't stop shivering.

"Why don't you go take a hot shower," Mindy suggested. "I can do dinner."

Bethann smiled. That was another one of the mom-isms. They'd grown up with a hot shower as the cure-all for everything: colds, flu, stomachache, depression. Her old bedroom and bathroom was now a guest room, but still felt like home. Persian Sun's photographs hung on the walls; the furniture was still the same, the curtains and bed linens. For a moment, she felt like she was sixteen again. She sat down on the bed and stared up at her favorite picture of Persian Sun. He was running in the pasture, his mane and forelock wild with the wind, his tail up in the air. He was so pretty. Tears sprang to her eyes.

Benjamin tapped on the door. "Can I come in?'

"Of course." Bethann wiped her eyes and chuckled. He could be so silly.

"This is weird," he said, entering tentatively. "Wife come stay in husband family house. No husband go to wife."

Bethann hugged him.

"Why are you crying?" he asked, touching her face gently.

"I don't know," she said, and motioned to the walls. "Persian Sun."

Benjamin nodded. "Is there somewhere else we can sleep?"

"No. It's not that bad. It's just been a long couple of days."

"Mindy is fine, Bethann. She is fine. Why do you worry?"

Bethann shrugged, tears welling up in her eyes again.

"Now, now," Benjamin said. "Go shower and get ready to eat. Mindy says she is making a great meal. She found frozen bread."

Bethann chuckled. "Do you want to come talk to me while I shower?" It was practically a nightly ritual.

Benjamin's eyes widened. "Is that allowed? Here in your father's house?"

Bethann laughed. "Of course, silly. This is America!"

Mindy had the table set and the food ready to lift out of the oven when they came downstairs. "Sit," she said, all proud of herself. Lasagna, garlic bread, and a pot of green tea awaited them. "We have dessert, too. Cheesecake. By the time we're ready for it, it'll be thawed."

~ 24 ~

Mindy had never seen so much snow, Bethann either for that matter. It was like living in Alaska and, at the moment, Bethann actually wished they did. That way she'd have nothing to do but sit inside the igloo, bundled up in fur (faux fur of course) and blankets. There was no doubt about it; she was coming down with a cold. She woke with a fever and chills.

"I'm fine, I'm fine," she kept insisting. "I'm fine." She must have said it at least five times during breakfast and three times on the way to the barn. Mrs. Butchling was already there. "That's odd." The roads were terrible, not to mention how the woman was never there this early, particularly on a weekday. She worked. She was a nurse.

Mindy half-expected to see her other eye black and blued. "Why does her husband hit her?"

Bethann shook her head. She'd forgotten all about explaining. "I'll tell you later," she said, shivering. When they entered the barn, Mrs. Butchling motioned from the back door for them to be quiet.

"Come see," she whispered. She'd already hayed the horses, so the horses were quiet. Malaki nickered at Mindy and Bethann and continued eating. "Look." Mrs. Butchling cracked open the back door a couple of inches. That was as far as she could get it to budge initially, without help, and that's when she'd first seen....

The deer were all curled up in the "deer bed" content as can be. Some were chewing hay; some had their eyes closed. Some had their heads resting on another's back or neck. Mindy searched for little Pixie Dust and almost panicked when she couldn't see her at first, what with all the deer and the snow. Then there she was, at her mother's side, a little fur ball...sound asleep. Her mother nuzzled her.

"Awe...." They closed the door softly and tiptoed halfway down the aisle way.

"Slowly...I...walk...step...by...step," Mindy said, exaggerating her every move.

Bethann shook her head. Admittedly, she was torn at this stage. They'd built the deer bed, and she was glad the deer were using it; they looked so warm and content, but then on the other hand. "Why are you here so early?" she asked Mrs. Butchling, for lack of anything better to say at the moment.

"I'll start the grain," Mindy said, walking away.

Graining the horses was a complicated process. Bethann said that in the old days, just about every horse ate the same thing. The only difference was the quantity, depending on their size, exercise level, and metabolism. And they all got the same supplement too, a squirt in each bucket of an all-purpose vitamin-mineral liquid on top of their grain, and a pinch of salt.

Now, for every horse, there was a different formula. Malaki for instance, as a base, only got oats, and barely a handful, because of her tendency to put on weight. She also got MSM crystals and vitamin pellets that included L-lysine. Patience got a small amount of sweet feed, along with an ounce of a liquid that contained glucosamine, chondroitin, and MSM. Andy got a scoop of sweet feed and oats mixed, along with a tablespoon of yucca. Legs got two scoops of a senior pellet and sweet feed mixture, and a powdered vitamin – mineral supplement. Rocky got a scoop and a half of sweet feed, along with every vitamin known to man and a digestive supplement. Dew Drop got two and a half scoops of the senior sweet feed – pellet mix, with a liquid vitamin. The list went on and on. It was the owner's responsibility to provide the supplements and prepare them. Each horse had its own vitamin drawer, vitamin shelf. Some of the horses got supplements twice a day, some just in the morning - some only in the evening. In addition to their base feed and vitamins, some got corn, some were allergic, some (the lightweights) got barley, some got beet pulp. They all got a little flax seed and bran. And they all got a pinch of mineral salt, even though they each had salt blocks in their stall, because some of the horses refused to lick them. Once this was all done, then it was time to dispense the medications. Most of the meds went into the feed. There was a chart that Bethann knew by heart.

"Go water," she told Mindy. And took over from there, with that same sad, angry look on her face - just like the other day when she'd talked to Mrs. Butchling.

"Did he hit her again?"

"Shhhh...."

Once the horses were grained and watered, it was time to feed the deer. Mindy threw the hay down from the hayloft. Mrs. Butchling helped her haul it to the back of the barn. Bethann mixed their grain and deer pellets. The three of them pushed and pounded and banged on the back doors and finally got them to open far enough for them to haul everything outside. That was about the time Bethann started sneezing.

The deer seemed intrigued with the sound, and would cock their heads one way then the other.

"You're talking their language," Mindy teased.

Bethann had to blow her nose, and that interested them even more. Pixie and the other two yearlings bucked and played and chased one another, happy as could be. A cozy night's rest brought new life to the does as well. Mindy watched them from a crack in the door. Every few minutes or so, one of them would raise their head and make a contented-sounding throaty noise, watching over the youngsters. And then another one would do the same thing.

Mindy flinched, startled when Mrs. Butchling walked up behind her.

"I'm sorry," the woman said.

Mindy took a good look at her and was happy to see she didn't have any more black and blue marks.

"Bethann went to lie down in the office. Do you want me to help you turn the horses out?"

"Don't you have to go to work?"

"No," Mrs. Butchling said, with the weight of the world in her voice. "Not today."

Mindy hesitated. "Are we going to turn them outside?"

"No, Bethann said just the arena."

Turning horses out in the winter was a chore in itself, let alone with all the blowing snow. Their stable blankets had to be removed and turnout blankets put on. Some had to have bell boots put on, to protect them from stepping on themselves if they got to playing too hard. One horse had to have a hock protector. One horse had to be done up in all fours, with fleece bandages. Some horses could be paired up - some had to go out alone. It was about a three-hour process of comings and goings, and at times, today, with Mindy and Mrs. Butchling barely holding on to the horses' lead ropes. The horses were all "higher than kites." If it weren't for the horses being just a little cautious about the footing to and from the arena, a few would have gotten loose for sure, Malaki being one of them. Not only was she literally feeling her oats, with all sorts of energy and wanting to play, she seemed to be hearing all sorts of scary things in the wind.

Bethann spent the entire time curled up on the couch in the office, shivering and sneezing and coughing, covered in a heavy horse blanket. When the stall-cleaning crew arrived at ten o'clock, the deer out back presented a problem. Mrs. Butchling brought Bethann a cup of tea. "What do you want the guys to do?"

Bethann sat up. "Uh...." She couldn't think.

"Do you want me to see if they can back the spreader in?" Usually they drove the spreader in the front door and out the back. Bethann nodded, staring into the cup. "Where's Mindy?"

"She's feeding the cats."

Mrs. Butchling left shortly thereafter. Not surprisingly, only one other boarder showed up at the barn all morning. It continued to snow, and snow, and snow. "This is ridiculous," Bethann said, raising her head to look out the window. It was unclear whether she was talking about the weather or being sick. She laid her head back down and closed her eyes. A few minutes later, Mindy heard her say, "My nose burns. I need Vitamin C."

Mindy phoned Yolanda; there was no answer. So she left a message, and phoned Becky. "We need food and Vitamin C, and some M&M's if you have any."

Both of their mothers responded to the call. Becky and Yolanda arrived bearing chicken noodle soup, casseroles, chewable and capsule forms of Vitamin C, and both peanut and plain M&M's. The soup was nice and hot. The casseroles could be heated up later.

Bethann thanked them dearly. "You didn't have to...."

"Peeshaw!" the one said.

"It's the least we can do."

Becky insisted on showing them the deer, but they were gone. All they got to see was the deer bed, and their tracks.

"You girls had better be careful," Yolanda's mom cautioned.

"We are. They're really gentle." It was a perfect afternoon. "Hurrah for snow days." They ate, they rode, they watched horse videos. They took turns checking on Bethann. They watched a kickboxing video. They ate some more. "Pass me the M&M's."

When it came time to feed in the evening, Bethann tried to gather some energy, but couldn't.

"Do you want some aspirin?"

"No," she replied, from under the blanket - to whoever had asked. "A fever is a good thing."

"Oh really?"

"Your sister is delirious," Yolanda told Mindy in the barn. Becky was haying and watering. Mindy was mixing feed.

"She just told me a fever is a good thing."

Mindy looked at her. "Oh, she always says that. She's not delirious."

"You gonna do the meds?"

"I'm gonna try." Mindy stared at the chart. The horses had heard the sound of grain being mixed and were getting impatient, Malaki in particular. "Be quiet," Mindy told her.

Malaki pinned her ears.

Mindy was afraid of making a mistake, giving one horse something that should have been given to another, and kept double-checking herself. Yolanda came up with an idea. She

101

wrote nametags on pieces of scratch paper for the horses needing meds, listing what they should get, and taped them to the inside of the grain buckets. It worked beautifully. When they were done feeding the horses, they peeked out back to see if the deer had returned. They had, so the girls prepared their food next.

When they opened the door, Pixie Dust scurried into the barn, the other two youngsters followed, and the three of them jogged down the aisle way. Pixie Dust decided to sample the horse's hay and picked of all stalls, Malaki's. Mindy hurried to get to the little deer and shoo her away, fearing Malaki would charge the stall gate, and if she could get close enough, bite the little deer. Before she got there, Malaki did begin to charge the gate, but then stopped and just stood there, as if seeing a ghost. Wide-eyed, she stretched her neck out and sniffed the little deer's back.

"Look how cute," Becky said.

Another sniff and Malaki squealed, sending all three of the young deer to the back door, as fast as their little legs could carry them.

The girls laughed. They were just too darling.

Pixie Dust stuck her head back in, as if testing the waters, and sneezed. "Ah choo."

It was still snowing.

~ 25 ~

Since it was the shortest distance to drive, and with more snow on the way, Bethann opted to stay at her parents' house again. She had Mindy call the students who hadn't phoned in already, and cancelled the night's lessons. They'd eaten all the food Becky and Yolanda's mother had brought, so dinner was up to Mindy again. She got very creative. She loved being home. She opened three cans of different types of soup; tomato, chicken noodle, and beef barley. She popped popcorn. She made tea. She made rice.

"What's the rice for?" Benjamin asked.

"For you."

He paused. "Thank you," he said, and tried some in his beef barley soup.

"The popcorn's good in the tomato."

He tried a little of that. "Hmmmmm…."

Bethann sat bundled up in blankets, sipping spoonfuls of chicken noodle soup broth.

When the phone rang, Mindy jumped up to get it.

"Mindy, it's Mom."

"Hi, Mom!"

"We heard about the storm and when no one answered Bethann's phone, I told your dad, I'll bet they're at the house."

"Yep, we're here."

Bethann shook her head no. She didn't want to talk on the phone. Her voice was all scratchy and she sounded terrible. Their mother would fly home instantly.

Mindy barely heard a word her mother was saying, for watching Bethann. "We're fine. We're all fine. Bethann, too."

Bethann rolled her eyes.

"We had your lasagna."

"Good. There's stroganoff and paprikash in the garage freezer."

"Where's Bethann…? Uh…." Mindy looked at her sister.

"No, no, NO!" she kept mouthing.

"She's in the bathroom. Um, I think she's going to be awhile." Mindy paused. "I don't know, just a feeling. Do you want to talk to Benjamin?"

Benjamin's eyes widened. "Me?"

Mindy handed him the phone.

"What am I to talk about?" he asked, covering the mouthpiece.

"I don't know. The weather."

It worked. He went on and on about the snow, never seen so much in my life, too much, too much - it's up to my knees, no, past my knees, pretty, yes, pretty, if you like snow, yes, more coming, lots, and before he hung up, "Okay, I will tell her. No need to come home."

Bethann looked at him. "Are they talking about coming home?"

"No. I only said that just in case."

Bethann sighed. He sure hadn't been very subtle. Mindy either.

"Do you know what you need," Mindy said, with a sudden revelation in regards to Bethann's misery. 'I don't know why I didn't think of this earlier. We have some at the barn."

"What?"

"Vicks."

Bethann smiled and then coughed.

Vicks was another Mom-ism choice.

When the phone rang again, all three of them thought it was their Mom calling back, somehow knowing, sensing that one of her children was ill, needing her. Mindy answered it and was surprised to learn otherwise. It was a local news station, Channel 4.

"We understand you've been taking care of some wild deer in this awful storm."

"Uh…." Mindy's protective instincts put her on guard.

"We'd like to send a camera crew out and take a picture of you feeding the deer."

"Who is it?" Bethann asked, seeing the blood draining from her little sister's face.

Mindy handed her the phone. She didn't want to talk to them. She didn't know what to say. She didn't want them taking her deer away. "It's a news station. They know about the deer."

"What?" Bethann shook her head. Oh lord, what next? She took the phone, said hello, and listened. It would just be a fifteen-second segment; they wanted to air it tomorrow night. They heard about it from a "little birdie." Would tomorrow morning at 8:00 be all right?

"Mindy has school tomorrow."

"No, she doesn't. West Geauga just cancelled. We're all set."

Bethann hung up the phone, dumbfounded.

"What? They're coming? Oh my God, what if they take them away?"

Bethann got up and walked out of the room. She needed to think. She needed to lie down.

Mindy chased after her. "I'm calling Dad."

"No, you're not! Don't you dare! We'll figure this out."

When Bethann closed the door behind her, Mindy flew back down the stairs and phoned Yolanda. "Get Becky on the phone." She declared, "It's an emergency."

Yolanda's phone had three-way dialing. They heard Mindy's news together.

"Wow! That is so cool!"

"No, it's not. What if they take them away?"

"Why would they take them away? It's a news station! What would they want with our deer?"

"I don't know."

"Who was it?"

Mindy had to think. "Jennifer Lynn."

"Oh, she's so cool! She does all kinds of animals. She likes animals."

"Which one is she?"

"The one with the spiked hair."

"When are they coming?"

"I don't know. Bethann didn't say."

"Well, go ask her."

"She's laying down."

"Ask her and call us back."

"I don't like this," Mindy said. She couldn't help but think of the raccoons. They were such a part of her life, and then they were gone. She never saw them again. "I don't like this at all."

Benjamin looked up from washing pots and pans when she came into the kitchen and handed her a towel. Mindy started drying.

"Don't worry," he said.

Mindy shrugged. She couldn't help it.

"It's just the local evening news 'obligatory animal story.' There is at least one on every show. It's all about ratings. They don't want your deer."

"I hope you're right," Mindy said.

Bethann never reappeared. She took a hot shower and rubbed her neck and chest with Vicks found in her mother's medicine cabinet, then went back into her old room, crawled into bed, and called it a night.

Mindy lay awake for hours, and finally fell asleep from worry and exhaustion. When the phone rang before they left for the barn the following morning, Mindy answered it. It was the camera crew, confirming the time and wanting the best directions from Cleveland.

"Directions?"

Bethann took the phone. Knowing Mindy, she'd send them to Pittsburgh. "No, it's no bother," she assured the man, bolstered by the fact that she wasn't feeling worse. She wasn't feeling better, but no worse was a good thing. She gave the man directions, confirmed the time, eight o'clock, and told them they would not be able to get very close to the deer, as they didn't want them frightened, the shorter the time there, the better.

Mindy nodded her approval. The man agreed as well. "That's okay with me, Ma'am. It's a little too chilly for a picnic."

Mindy phoned Becky and Yolanda; their mothers would drop them off. Both girls were excited. Even Mindy at this point, was starting to get into it. She hoped Pixie Dust sneezed for the camera. The little deer was so cute when she did that. Oh no, but what if they think she's sick, and won't listen when we tell them that's how they talk? What if they think she has something contagious?

Bethann looked at her, seeing the weight of the world on her fourteen-year-old shoulders. "It'll be all right, I promise. If we said no, Mindy, it would probably have caused alarm. They'd wonder what we were hiding. This way they can come take their picture, then leave, and that's that."

"I hope so." Mindy sighed.

"You'll see. A week from now we'll be laughing about how concerned we were."

"Why a week from now? I want to laugh about it tonight."

"Okay, we'll laugh about it tonight."

~ 26~

There was a total of sixteen inches of snow on the ground that morning with no sign of letting up. Maple Dale looked like a mirage from the top of the hill, the snow blowing and billowing in the spotlights. It reminded Bethann of the winter after Leah Oliver died...the bitter cold, the emptiness.

"And God bless us everyone," Mindy said, when they made it to the barn.

Bethann smiled. With all the hopes and wishes going through her mind at this moment, foremost she did not want her little sister's heart broken. Losing something, someone, is never easy. But with the extent to which Mindy cared, every loss was paramount. She wished their mother and father were home. "Don't forget to practice your violin this week," she said to Mindy, seemingly out of the blue.

Mindy nodded, the furthest thing from her mind at the moment. Malaki whinnied when she heard their car doors slam shut. Food. Breakfast. The barn doors were easier to open today, and there was a message on the blackboard. "I hayed already," it read. "Hope you're feeling better."

Bethann stared at it, as if seeing a ghost.

"Gees. What time does she start work?" Mindy asked.

"Who?"

"Mrs. Butchling."

"Oh...." Bethann heaved an internal sigh of relief. "Um...I'm not sure."

"I can feed, if you just want to go in the office."

"No, that's okay," Bethann said, shivering. "I'm fine."

Mindy wanted to check on the deer, but it was still dark, and she wouldn't be able to see out back unless she opened the doors and had the lights shining. No sense doing that until they were ready to feed them. She helped Bethann mix grain for the horses, and then started watering.

"This is a good idea," she heard Bethann say.

"What?"

"The lists on the buckets."

"Yolanda did that. It worked really well."

When watering the horses down at the far end, Mindy tiptoed to the back door and listened, hoping to hear some rustling in the straw, some crunching in the snow, breathing, sneezing, anything.

Nothing.

The deer either weren't there or were all still sleeping. Growing apprehensive again, Mindy half-hoped they actually had moved on and were gone, in another county, another state, happy as can be, South maybe, where it was warmer. She heard water running and turned. "Oh, shoot." She was overflowing Dew Drop's water bucket. She opened his stall gate and kicked sawdust under it to soak up the water. "Sorry," she told him, and patted him on the head. "You're such a nice horse." He pushed against her hand. "And so pretty." He wasn't really. He was too big to be considered *pretty*. He stood about 17.2. Handsome maybe. Yes, handsome, she thought, and always so well groomed, so shiny, so friendly.

Becky and Yolanda arrived then, all excited. Their enthusiasm was contagious.

"Shhhh," Bethann told them. "If you get the deer going and they start pounding on the back door, they'll look aggressive."

"Good point."

When they finished graining the horses, she had them all go to the office to wait. "The less noise, the better," she said, herding them along.

"But shouldn't we go see if they're there."

"No. If they're not, then so be it."

Bethann put on water for tea, and took the opportunity to lie down for a few minutes. The girls sounded like magpies. "What'll we say? What'll we do? You talk. No, you. Can you believe this? It's so cool. I wonder how they heard about us? I don't know. Who cares! We're gonna be on TV!" And then ultimately, "They're here!"

Bethann stopped the girls at the door. "Wait. Just wait," she said, and had a coughing fit. "Mindy, go turn off the stove." More coughing. "Yolanda, does your mom know you're wearing makeup?"

"Yes...sort of."

She looked at Becky. "Don't you think you should wear a hat?"

"What? I spent an hour on my hair."

They all laughed.

"Okay," Bethann said, and opened the door. "It's Showtime!"

The girls were all aflutter. They'd never seen a celebrity up close before. Jennifer Lynn was even prettier in person, so glamorous, and so very nice. "I love animals," she said, petting the horses while her cameraman went over the lay of the land.

"If I could be inside," he said, coming in all snow covered. "It would be better."

"I'm concerned you might frighten them," Bethann cautioned. She'd hoped he'd film them from the top of the hill.

"Sorry, but we can't. It's too cold and too far away," he said.

Inside, it would have to be.

"All right, so what do you normally do?" Jennifer Lynn asked, rubbing her gloved hands together.

"Well, first we hay them then we grain them," Becky said, looking right into the camera.

"Or sometimes the other way around," Yolanda added, "depending on where they are and how hungry they are."

Jennifer Lynn smiled. "Why don't you act like I'm not here, though obviously I am," she said, chuckling. "And we'll try and play it by ear. How's that?"

Everyone agreed. The cameraman filmed the girls mixing the deer's feed, filmed them throwing down the hay from the loft and hauling it down the aisle way, filmed them opening the doors, or at least trying to open the doors. Bethann gave them a hand. Mindy was quiet as a mouse, and so pale. Bethann actually feared she might faint - or puke, one or the other. When they finally got the doors to budge, the cameraman zoomed in. Jennifer Lynn stepped close.

There stood the deer, waiting patiently; four does and the three yearlings. "Wow," Jennifer Lynn whispered. "My gosh, they're beautiful."

Pixie Dust advanced first as usual, the other two youngsters followed.

Mindy smiled proudly - still quiet, still pale, but smiling. The girls cleared away two spots and dumped the grain. Jennifer Lynn was talking into her microphone, calling the girls Angels of Mercy. She nodded for them to continue, so they hauled out the hay. At this point, Pixie Dust, mouth full and tail swishing, jogged past them into the barn.

Malaki stuck her head out of her stall and whinnied.

Pixie Dust sneezed, and jogged down the aisle way and back, the other two yearlings following and swish - swishing their tails.

"They are soooo precious," Jennifer Lynn kept saying.

Swish, swish. Ah choo. Ah choo.

Malaki whinnied, watching them. Legs nickered, and then so did Andy. One by one, all of the horses came to the front of their stalls, straining their necks to see. Pixie Dust marched up to Mindy, looking and waiting, head tilted one way, then the other. Mindy smiled. She wanted to be petted. Mindy stroked her head and then her neck. Yolanda fed her some grain, Becky too. And all the while, Jennifer Lynn talked, as the camera rolled. Whenever she asked a question, one of the girls had the answer. One of the other yearlings got brave and horned in on the act. It suddenly wanted to be petted, too.

The cameraman filmed all this, and then filmed the does, eating calmly, but with watchful motherly eyes. When he stepped behind the yearlings to get a close-up of them, Bethann motioned for him to stay back. One of the does turned away and walked over to the deer bed and lay down. He filmed this too, a close-up, zoom, closer. The doe looked so pretty just lying there.

"Is she the mom?"

"No," Yolanda said. "She's the one we think is pregnant."

"Wow!" Jennifer Lynn said, sighing as she glanced at her watch. "I hate to leave. I could stay here and watch them forever."

As if on cue and knowing the visit was over, the little deer marched outside, pushing and playing. Bethann closed the doors.

"I'd like one more shot of you girls," Jennifer Lynn said. The three of them instinctively draped their arms across one another's shoulders and smiled for the camera.

"Okay, that's a wrap," the cameraman said, having fun and being a bit theatrical for their benefit. "Thank you."

Bethann walked them out. As they passed Malaki's stall, she did that "biting the air" thing she did on occasion when something didn't suit her fancy or she wasn't getting enough attention. When the cameraman ducked out of her way, she wheeled in her stall and bucked and squealed.

~ 27 ~

It was the longest day in the girls' lives, ever. Out of boredom, they decided to clean the observation room. It wasn't that dirty, so that didn't take long. They ran the sweeper, they dusted, they stacked the magazines, they updated the bulletin board. They cleaned the kitchen next. That took about a half hour. They did foot races in the arena at one point. Becky was the fastest.

"Don't get sweaty," Bethann warned.

They watched TV. They watched videos.

"Let's go see if *someone* brought more apples." The girls bundled up to go outside.

"Don't go near the deer," Bethann said.

"We won't."

"And follow your tracks back. That way you won't get lost."

"Yes, Mom," the girls said.

"I'm serious. If you get lost, you're on your own."

"Yeah, right." The girls laughed.

"Maybe we'll walk to the house," Mindy said.

"No." Bethann pointed a finger at her. "Don't even think about it."

"Oh my God," Mindy said. "Now you even look like Mom."

The girls headed out and around the arena. Bethann needn't worry. They weren't going to walk to the house. After being in the nice warm observation room for hours, and the wind blowing out of the northwest, the direction they were taking, they were lucky to make it down the hill.

"Come on," Mindy said. "It's just a little further."

The effort paid off. There in the clearing, just before the big oak, lay a fresh supply of apples. And the only tracks they could see, coming and going, were deer tracks.

"Oh my God," Yolanda said. "I bet it is Leah Oliver."

The girls looked up at the trees and all around, amidst an eerie silence. Becky stuck her tongue out and ate some snow.

"Look." She pointed to one of the trees where an owl watched their every move.

"Let's go back," Yolanda said. "This is creepy."

On the way up the hill, they heard a siren in the distance, growing louder and louder, then more sirens. As they rounded the end of the arena, they saw Bethann standing outside the observation room, apparently awaiting their return. "The power's out," she said, when they got closer. "It's out all over the development."

"What are we going to do?" Yolanda asked.

"Nothing, for the moment," Bethann said, hurrying them along. "We'll just have to try and stay warm. I lit a fire in the wood burner. I don't want you girls to get chilled."

"Wow! When did you get so old?" Mindy asked.

"Come on," Bethann said. "Get inside. Now."

At first being without power was fun. They sat around the fire, talking, laughing, reliving the morning. "Oh no! What if it doesn't come back on by six?" They'd miss the news broadcast.

"It will, don't worry," Bethann said.

Mindy smiled. Now that sounded like her sister and not her mom.

"Good thing we heated up the paprikash earlier."

They all nodded. At least they weren't hungry. Plus, there were always the vending machines. Several times during the afternoon, the fact crossed Mindy's mind that Howard her cousin – not really her cousin, was supposed to come over this evening at seven-thirty for their tutoring session.

"What'll we do about watering the horses?" Becky asked.

Bethann opened her eyes. She'd been catnapping. "We have a generator. I'll get it going, no problem."

Becky's and Yolanda's mothers were both at work and were planning to pick them up on their way home around seven. No one showed up for lessons, no mail was delivered. No blacksmith arrived, though two were scheduled. No veterinarians out and about stopped in while making rounds. No boarders came. Not even Mrs. Butchling. It was as if they were cut off from the rest of the world entirely.

Again, Bethann thought of Leah's lonely winter here, all by herself, no friends, no family. She dozed and woke to the smell of popcorn popping in the microwave. It took a moment for things to register in her mind. The lights were on. "When did the power come back on?"

"Around four-thirty," Mindy said.

"What time is it now?"

"Five forty-five. We were going to wake you in a little while."

Yolanda brought her a cup of tea. "We called the station. They said they'll be "airing the deer piece" around six-twenty. We called everybody we know and told them."

"Cool." Bethann sat up and sipped her tea. "Thank you. I'll drink this and we'll go feed."

"It's already done," Becky said.

"The meds too?"

Mindy nodded. "We're good, huh?"

Bethann smiled. "Yes."

Becky brought her popcorn. "Don't worry. It's the non-buttered version."

"Wow, I don't know what to say. I'm overwhelmed."

The girls chuckled. It was nice being able to do something for her for a change.

"Uh," Yolanda said. "Could you maybe tell us a little about Leah Oliver, since we like, don't have anything to do for a few minutes."

Mindy looked at Yolanda, couldn't believe she said that, then looked at Bethann. She'd obviously wanted to ask herself, but....

"She was really nice," Bethann said. "We all really liked her. You all would have, too. She was an awesome instructor." She looked at Becky. "Though, she would have had a fit watching you dismount."

The girls laughed. Becky had this horrible absentminded habit of having one foot practically on the ground before taking the other one out of the remaining stirrup. She knew the correct way to dismount, raise the right leg up and over the saddle, hold onto the pummel and back of the saddle, and remove both feet from the stirrups and lower yourself to the ground. But every once in a while, she'd be thinking of something else, and.... Bethann shivered.

"Do you think she could still be here?" Yolanda asked.

Again, Mindy looked from one to the other. Becky, too.

"I don't know," Bethann said. "Not if you read about how ghosts react and considering the time she's been gone. You guys weren't even born yet, that's how long ago it was."

All three girls started telling her about the apples with the "no tracks anywhere" and the video, how it looked as if Leah was there that day at Bethann's show.

"Did you ever see it? It's right at the beginning."

Bethann shook her head. "I don't watch it much. I need another horse," she said, which didn't make a whole lot of sense to any of them but Mindy. "Maybe I'll watch it when I get home some day, if it ever stops snowing."

The girls laughed.

"Will you tell us then, if you see her?" Yolanda asked.

Bethann nodded.

It was six o'clock.

Mindy turned the television on and they all sat waiting. There were three commercial breaks in the first fifteen minutes, and nothing but bad news in between, murders, robberies, natural disasters, embezzlement, fights in the schools and in the courtrooms.

"When we return, we'll take you to a farm in Geauga County where the deer and the antelope play. Stay tuned, you won't want to miss this." Before they panned away, they showed a preview of all the deer looking into the barn.

The girls clapped and screamed. "That's them! That's them!" They could hardly sit through the following commercials, five of them to be exact. One was for feminine products, one promoting a drug for advanced-age sexual performance, two for pain relievers, and one for youthful skin. When each one faded out, their expectations rose and fell. Finally, the news came back on.

"Yes!"

"With Geauga County seeing one of the worst winters on record...." It was Jennifer Lynn.

"We know her!" Becky said.

All of them laughed

"Shhh.... Shhhh...."

"It's a challenge for anyone to stay warm, let alone the animals."

Bethann and the girls watched mesmerized. They were feeding the deer, petting the deer. The horses were looking on. "Animals in the wild have survival instincts we humans don't have. They know when it's going to rain. They know when it's going to snow. And apparently they know who they can trust to care for them when times get hard."

"You have to be careful what you feed them. They have sensitive stomachs," Becky said. "They need a balanced diet."

"These are does and yearlings," Yolanda said. "At first we thought the yearlings were still fawns, but their spots are gone, so they had to have been born last year. They're just small, probably about eight months old or so."

"They become yearlings officially when they survive their first winter."

"They're Whitetail Deer."

"We feed them twice a day."

"How long have you been feeding them?"

"A couple of weeks now."

Little Pixie Dust ran up and down the aisle, the other two yearlings frolicking along behind her.

"It's a deer bed. It shelters them from the wind."

"It's amazing how they trust you."

"We had to earn their trust," Mindy said.

The camera followed the doe as she walked to the deer bed and lay down. When she looked up, the camera zoomed in on her in slow motion, her eyes as soft as a breeze. Snowflakes lit gently upon her eyelashes. "This doe will be giving birth soon, in the harshest reality of late winter. But in Geauga County at Maple Dale Farm, tonight…there is room at the inn." The deer laid her head to rest on the straw. "I'm Jennifer Lynn, WPVZ, Channel 4 news."

~ 28 ~

The girls were extremely pleased; even Mindy sat happy as can be. "I wish we could have taped it. I want to watch it again."

"Don't worry, they'll probably run it again tonight," Bethann said. "We can tape it then."

"Wow, can you believe the doe, and how she laid her head down just when Jennifer Lynn said that about the inn." Becky got up for more popcorn.

"I know. That was amazing," Yolanda said.

Editing, Bethann thought, but kept that to herself. It was done beautifully. No wonder they all had tears in their eyes at the end. She drew a breath and sighed. "Did it snow all afternoon?"

"Yes."

The phone started ringing, and never stopped. Just about every one of their boarders phoned to say they saw the news, and how exciting it was to see the girls and Maple Dale on TV. The only one they didn't hear from was Mrs. Butchling.

Mindy asked about her in the car on the way home.

"It's not what you're thinking, Mindy. Her husband doesn't know he hits her."

"What?"

"He has Alzheimer's. She had to have him committed yesterday. He's only sixty years old."

"Oh how sad."

"They had such a good marriage. She loves him so much," Bethann said, her bottom lip quivering with that last declaration. "Life is so tragic sometimes."

Mindy nodded. "How long has he had it?"

"The last couple of years. She's been trying to take care of him herself. She promised him she wouldn't put him in a home." Bethann's voice cracked. "In the beginning, he knew."

Mindy didn't know what to say. "Are you all right?"

"I don't know," Bethann said, wiping her eyes. She turned into the drive at their parents' house and pulled up next to the garage. "She's going to have to sell Dew Drop."

"What? Why?"

"Finances."

"Can't we let her board for free?"

"I offered. But she needs the money she can get from selling him."

"Oh God, that's sucks!"

Bethann looked at her.

"I'm sorry, but it does!"

Bethann nodded. "Just don't say anything to her, okay. She doesn't want anyone to know until it happens. She doesn't want to talk about it."

"Okay." The two of them stared out the windshield into the falling snow.

"Why don't *you* buy him," Mindy said.

Bethann shrugged. "It's hard, Mindy," she said, tears welling up in her eyes. "He's not for me, he belongs to her."

Mindy understood and started crying as well.

"I'm s-sorry," Bethann said.

Mindy nodded.

"You were having such a good day."

"It doesn't matter." Dew Drop loved Mrs. Butchling. She could tell. "It's not fair."

"I know."

Mindy sat there, wiping her eyes and crying harder. "I miss Mom."

"Me, too."

"This sucks!"

Benjamin pulled in behind them, smiling at usual. Time to put on a happy face. "I bring dinner to your father's house," he said, when they opened the doors and got out. He'd picked up an assortment of take-out Chinese food. "No MSG."

Bethann and Mindy followed behind him, their Pied Piper. At home, Benjamin's favorite place to eat was the living room floor in front of the fireplace. Why not here, too,

Bethann thought, and spread a blanket while Mindy lit the fire. Benjamin heard all about the highlights of their day.

"My day," he said. "Was not so good."

Bethann stared. She'd never known him to have a bad day. "It is true," he said, refusing to elaborate. Bethann smiled. This was a good thing. She didn't realize until right this instant, how much pressure he put on her being so happy all the time with nothing but good in his world. It was not as if she walked on eggshells around him, she certainly did not. But she did have this nagging feeling in the back of her mind, always, that some day if something were "not so good" as Benjamin put it, it would be catastrophic. The end.

"I even walked backwards all afternoon to see if my luck would change. Bump into this, bump into that."

Bethann and Mindy laughed. "I think you make this stuff up," Bethann said.

"Ah so," he said, bowing at the waist.

"Thank you," Bethann said, for the laugh. She appreciated it. She needed it.

Mindy, too. "Thank you."

"I see tracks of tears," he said, cupping Bethann's face in his hands. "If I can make you laugh, when you want to cry, my day is good."

"But what about when I need to cry."

"Then cry good," he said, nodding. "Only not now. Now you eat."

They all laughed.

"Where's cousin Howard?" Benjamin asked.

"I don't know," Mindy said. It wasn't like him to be late. He was usually early in fact. "You know, he's really not our cousin. He's more like just a friend of the family."

"Oh?" Benjamin stuffed his mouth full of Chinese noodles. "How so?"

When Mindy shrugged he looked at Bethann? "Why do we call him cousin Howard?"

Bethann shrugged as well, and the doorbell rang then. They knew it was Howard, who else would it be? He stepped into the foyer looking like the Abominable Snowman. There was no car leaving the drive.

"Did you walk?"

"Yes," he said, trying not to shiver. "My mom wasn't home yet."

"Here, give me your jacket," Bethann said, shaking her head. No hat, no gloves. "Go sit by the fire."

Benjamin looked up and smiled. "Ahhh, it is friend-of-the-family, Howard."

Mindy laughed.

"Did you have dinner?"

"Yes," Howard said. "Thank you."

Mindy studied him. He looked taller, grown up. Then again, she was sitting on the floor. She wolfed down the rest of her noodles and got up and took her plate into the kitchen. When she came back into the living room, Howard was explaining *how* he wasn't related. Benjamin must have asked.

"You ready?" She turned to go upstairs to her room. Howard followed.

Benjamin stopped them. "Leave door open," he said. "Asian rule."

Mindy blushed. Howard, too.

"Did you want some hot chocolate?" Bethann asked.

Howard hesitated, thinking. "Coffee would be nice."

"Coffee coming right up," Bethann said, with a chuckle. "Get it? Coming right up. I'll be bringing it upstairs."

Mindy rolled her eyes – a sudden roll reversal, she being the grownup.

Howard had never had coffee in his life, and it showed. When Bethann brought it up, he took that first sip. "It's delicious," he said, looking like he had a mouthful of muck. "Thank you."

"Did you want cream and sugar?"

"No, this is fine. Thank you." Another sip.

"Did you see the news?" Mindy asked, when Bethann had gone.

"No," he said, putting the mug down. He reached for her algebra book.

"Do you think we'll have school tomorrow?"

"I hope not," he said. "My buddies and I want to go snowboarding again."

"You snowboard?"

"Yes, why wouldn't I?"

"I don't know." Mindy just looked at him, and then didn't look at him again during the entire tutoring session. The hour passed quickly.

"Your mom's here," Bethann called up the stairs.

"Watch Channel 4 news tonight at eleven," Mindy told him. He promised he would.

~ 29 ~

By nine-thirty that night, school closings started scrolling across the bottom of the television screen. The first two times through the alphabet, West Geauga Schools were not listed. Mindy crossed her fingers. They were usually the last to cave in. Third time was the charm. There it was. "Yes!" Yolanda and Becky were watching for it at their houses. The three were on the phone almost immediately, planning the day ahead.

Food was at the top of the list - who would bring what and how much. They decided they should bake cookies at the barn. They could bake them in the morning and have them for after their ride. They also decided they should make two batches, so each could take some home. All three checked their kitchen cupboards to make sure they had the ingredients needed; chocolate chips being number one. Mindy had a pack and so did Yolanda.

"Do we want walnuts?"

"For the one batch, sure."

They were all set.

"I hope I can stay awake till eleven," Becky said.

"Me, too." Yolanda yawned.

All three would be sound asleep when the news station aired the "deer segment" again. It came on just before they signed off at midnight. The only person the girls knew, their age, still awake, was Howard. When Bethann and Mindy arrived at the barn the following morning, there were five cars there waiting for them, and Mrs. Butchling.

She motioned for Bethann and Mindy to come into the barn quickly, and closed the doors behind them. "These people are nuts! I told them to go away and they won't! They want to see the deer."

"Oh my." Bethann had feared as much and set out, "to nip this in the bud immediately." Mindy was right on her heels. "Go back inside."

"No, you're sick. My voice is better."

"Mindy, now!" Bethann said.

By then all the people there were out of their cars and advancing. "We just want to see the deer."

"But you'll frighten them. It took us a long time to get them used to *us*."

"We'll be quiet," said one of the women, carrying a toddler.

"Ma'am, please, all of you. Please…just g-go home."

"But I saw the Virgin Mary."

"What?"

"In the manger, in the deer bed."

"The deer aren't here!" Mindy yelled, from the barn. "They're gone!"

"See." Bethann was polite, but firm. "Please…. Go home."

A few walked to their cars and left, some just stood there, fast becoming snow covered and shivering. Bethann closed the barn doors behind her. "Are they leaving?"

Mrs. Butchling peeked out the window and shook her head. "I want to go strangle that woman with the baby. I had to practically kick her out of the barn."

"I knew we shouldn't have gone on the news," Mindy said.

"Whose idea was it?" Mrs. Butchling asked.

"I don't know," Bethann said, coughing. "They called us. We didn't call them."

"Is this private property?" Mrs. Butchling asked.

"Yes, why?" Bethann owned it.

"I think we should post a no trespassing sign. I can get me a gun and stand up there and say 'Get off my land.' I've always wanted to do that."

Mindy laughed. She didn't know Mrs. Butchling could be so funny, and with so many problems of her own yet. Bethann ventured another look. The "trespassers" were leaving. "Thank God."

Mindy opened the back doors and surveyed the deer tracks. "They've been here recently," she said. The fresh snow sat high on their hoof prints. There were human prints also, a man's judging from the size. "Look. See how big?"

Bethann marveled at her, so confident and so knowing at such a young age.

"I'm going to follow them," Mindy said, standing up with her hand over her brow and staring due west – like some kind of Sacagawea, Indian guide.

"What?" Bethann shook her head. "No way!"

"Why not? I just want to see where they go."

"I said no! Now get in here!"

Mrs. Butchling had already hayed and watered. She was late for work, but said she wasn't going to leave the barn unattended. Bethann thanked her and walked her to her car for an update on her husband. Mindy started mixing the grain.

Malaki watched her.

"You're awfully quiet," Mindy said, looking at her.

She twitched her ears. She didn't pin them. She just twitched them. That was unlike her.

"What's the matter?"

Malaki just looked at her.

Becky arrived then, and a minute or two later, Yolanda.

"Who are those people out there?"

"Oh no," Mindy said. "Are there more? They're here to see the deer. They scared them away."

"You mean they're gone?"

Mindy and Becky nodded.

"Forever?"

Mindy shrugged.

Bethann came into the barn and bolted the doors behind her. "Maybe they shouldn't have said which farm."

"Do you think the herd will come back?" Yolanda asked.

"I don't know, probably, maybe. Who knows? Maybe if the people would just leave." Bethann sighed in exasperation and that brought on another coughing fit. "You'd swear they'd never seen a deer before." She shook her head, finished dispensing the medications, and the girls helped feed. They took turns checking every so often to see if the deer had returned, and grew gloomier and gloomier as time went on.

"We didn't even get to tell them good-bye," Becky said, at one point.

"Don't say that."

"Do you want to make cookies?"

"No."

"Me neither."

Bethann glanced at them from her desk in the office, assessing the whole situation. This had been going to happen sooner or later anyway. The deer couldn't stay forever, nor would they want to. When spring arrived.... But that's just it, she told herself. It hasn't arrived and it's cold. And it's snowing, and it's never going to stop snowing, not at this rate.

Two more unfamiliar cars pulled in. "Enough," she said. "Enough." She bundled up and went out and talked to the people, then headed for the hayloft. There were two old wooden sawhorses stored way in the back. She dragged them out of the loft and down the hill, hoisted them onto her car trunk, and drove them to the top of the main driveway.

"Where'd you go?" Mindy asked, when she returned.

"I blocked the road," she said, lying down on the couch in her office. "Call everyone and tell them."

"Call who?"

"Everyone," Bethann said, closing her eyes.

"Okay...."

Mindy, Yolanda, and Becky took turns phoning all the boarders to let them know. "No, you can move the barricade. Just put it back once you get in."

Most everyone said they weren't planning on coming today anyway, with the latest weather development. The girls turned the television on. The forecast: six more inches of snow by morning. The girls decided to ride to take their mind off the absent deer. With the three of them gone and the lounge and observation room totally quiet, Bethann fell into a deep sleep. She dreamt she was driving to go visit her mom, but realized halfway there, that she was going to their old house. Worried that she'd be late, she decided to fly instead, and elevated herself high in the sky. She looked down and was soaring over a cornfield. She could see hunters, their rifles aimed. "Don't kill the deer," she said, in a loud voice, and woke herself up with her voice echoing in the room.

She had a fever. It was spiking. She looked into the arena, saw the girls riding, and closed her eyes. Oh, Leah, she thought. If only you *could* fix things. Bring the deer back. We'll get them to move on when the weather breaks. It's just too cold out there right now. They need us.... She thought of Mrs. Butchling. And I think we need them.

When she woke again, it was to the delicious smell of chocolate chip cookies, hot out of the oven.

"They're back," Mindy announced, when Bethann appeared before them. "They're back! They're eating! They're back!"

Yolanda and Becky nodded confirmation.

"They're back!"

~ 30 ~

The girls decided to go ahead and make the "No Trespassing" sign Mrs. Butchling had suggested and attach it to one of the sawhorses. Bethann received a phone call from Jennifer Lynn while they were gone. She said she was just checking in to see how the deer were doing, and to find out if the girls and Bethann liked the story.

"We loved it," Bethann said. "But unfortunately...." She told her about the people showing up and the deer being scared away.

"Oh my." Jennifer Lynn sighed. "We've gotten several calls too, I was afraid of this."

"Did any of them say anything about seeing the Virgin Mary?"

"Yes, and I've watched the clip twice now, and have no idea what they are referring to. I don't see it."

Good, Bethann thought. "Would we be able to p-purchase a copy of the 'clip'?" Not one of them had set their recorders to tape the show. They thought they'd be awake to do it.

"Of course, I'll send you one. I apologize for any...."

"It's okay. It's not your fault." Bethann thanked her and hung up. The girls should have been back by this time. She decided she'd better go check on them. It was snowing even harder now. She bundled up, teeth chattering.

"Oh wonderful." The girls were in the barn, and had Pixie Dust and the other two yearlings inside with them. Pixie Dust's dam was half in and half out the back door way, content with watching.

"Where's the pregnant one?" Bethann asked.

"In the deer bed."

"We're afraid to leave them," Yolanda said. "Do you suppose anyone would harm them?"

"I don't think so," Bethann said, petting Pixie Dust.

Sneeze, sneeze. Ah choo. Ah choo.

All the horses stood at the front of their stalls, quietly watching. The barn was like a cocoon, a blanket of snow protecting it, protecting them...from the rest of the world.

"Not intentionally at least. This isn't hunting season." Bethann thought about her dream. She was glad there were no cornfields around. And that it was snowing; there was no snow in her dream. Another place, another time.

"We were thinking," Mindy said.

Oh no, Bethann thought, sniffling.

"What if we could get them into the stall with the sawdust? There's hardly any left, we wouldn't be wasting much." The sawdust stall was at the back of the barn.

Bethann shook her head.

"Just for at night. And it would only be until the weather breaks. It can't snow forever."

Bethann turned to walk away.

"We're not even sure we can get them to come in, and we won't leave one out. They'd all have to come in or none, because they're a herd, and that's why we think if one of the adults comes in, the others will follow and...."

Bethann sighed.

"Please...."

All three girls steepled their hands as if praying.

"Please...."

"I'm leaving in ten minutes. I called your moms and told them I'd drop you off."

Was that a yes? The girls looked at one another. Yes!

"Get some more grain," Becky said.

Pixie Dust followed Mindy into the feed room. The other two yearlings were right on her heels but stayed outside the door. Malaki stretched her neck to try and reach them. Becky and Yolanda opened the back doors wider. Pixie Dust's dam backed out then came back in halfway again. One of the other does appeared at her side. The girls pried opened the doors a little wider.

"This is as far as they'd come," Yolanda told Mindy when she returned with the grain – Pixie Dust and the two yearlings following. "They're suspicious. Remember what we read. Deer don't like confinement. Even if we can get them into the stall...."

Mindy shrugged. "Once they're in, there in. The stalls are built for horses that are bigger and stronger than them. What harm can they do?"

Yolanda shook her head. "I'm just reminding you."

All three girls had butterflies in their stomachs.

"Should we get some hay?"

"Probably."

Becky went to get a bale, and as they waited and petted Pixie Dust and the other two yearlings, Yolanda and Mindy heard a noise behind them, and turned slowly. Two of the does were all the way in the barn, and another one right behind them. Being up this close to the yearlings was one thing, the does, quite another. The girls were sandwiched in. Any sudden move and it could be a disaster.

Mindy looked at Malaki. Don't you dare squeal, don't you dare. "Good girl," she started saying, that reverse psychology thing. "Good girl...good girl...good girl...."

Becky broke open the hay bale, spread it in the stall over the sawdust, and stepped out and around the deer very quietly. Mindy led Pixie Dust into the stall then and the other two yearlings followed. When Mindy put the grain down, they started eating. The three does stepped forward, looking and listening, watching their every move.

"We've got to get the other one."

Becky edged her way to the back door. The pregnant doe was still in the deer bed.

"Maybe walk around behind it," Mindy suggested.

"Okay," Becky said, willing to give it a try. She trudged out into the snow. The three does inside the barn turned and watched her, looking indecisive, stay in or go back out. Stay in....

Becky slid twice and fell, not that she had that far to fall. The snow was up to her thighs. "Come on, Mommy," she said, softly. "Come inside with your friends. See, they want you to come. You're worrying them."

The doe looked at her. She appeared comfortable right where she was, and none too interested in moving.

"I hope she's not in labor," Mindy said.

"Don't say that."

"Well, it is a possibility."

Becky climbed through the snow to get a little closer. "Come on," she said. "Let's go. Come on."

"Is she moving?"

"She's thinking about it."

The doe straightened her front legs, stretched, and then laid back down.

"Come on, girl. You can do it."

The doe stood and shook off the snow.

"Here she comes," Becky said, sitting back in the snow to get out of her way. Yolanda stood ready to close the door once she came in. The doe hesitated entering. She looked up the aisle way at the other deer, then up at the ceiling, at the horses...at Yolanda. Becky climbed through the snow behind her. "Come on, girl. You can do it," she kept saying, waiting and waiting. "Come on, girl. Please. I'm freezing my butt off out here."

The doe took a big bold step, then another, and finally, was inside. The rest of the herd had eaten most of the feed, but the hay all spread out looked very appetizing to this particular doe. That's where she was headed. Without an apparent second thought, she walked right into the stall and started eating. Mindy bent down to see if the doe was "bagging up," getting milk. She nodded.

"I'm no expert, but I'd say she's getting close."

Two of the does walked lazily up the aisle way.

"We need more grain."

Yolanda and Becky pulled the back doors closed. It took some pushing and shoving. In that short bit of time they had them open, snow had accumulated on the barn floor. They latched the doors tight.

The horses seemed rather intrigued by this turn of events, though not overly concerned. They'd seen the deer before and, after all, deer or no deer, first and foremost the deer were fellow animals and not predator animals. Malaki nickered when the one doe got close, and it stopped, turning its head one way then the other. Malaki snorted and sniffed. "Come over here and talk to me," she kept insisting, in that Malaki way of hers.

Becky got more feed and by shaking the can, led them back down the aisle way. They followed along, calm as can be, necks stretched and trying to get close to the feed, but from a safe distance. The youngsters had gotten their fill and starting rooting in the hay. Like dominoes then, one, two, three, they lay down and curled up in comfortable little balls.

The stall seemed small now, maybe too small. "Nah, they all fit in the deer bed," Mindy said, sounding like an old farmer. "They'll be fine."

The second doe entered the stall, sniffed the two yearlings, and started eating hay. That just left Pixie Dust's dam and the other doe. They were reluctant to enter. It was hard to tell if they were afraid. They didn't appear to be. They just wouldn't enter.

Yolanda and Mindy clasped hands and started edging them along. "Don't get crazy," Becky said, still holding the feed can and watching their eyes.

"Come on…. Come on…."

It was so tempting to nudge them, but the girls knew better. If deer spooked anything like horses, they'd charge forward and run Becky over. "It's okay, there you go. It's okay."

Becky started turning as the one entered, her back to the front of the stall, still shaking the grain can, eyes on the deer.

"Dump it in the middle," Mindy said.

Becky drew her hand back slowly, and poured the grain in a little pile. Pixie Dust's mom was the last to enter, looking around and not so sure. When Mindy and Yolanda drew a little closer, the doe walked into the stall and Becky backed out. All in.

Slowly, very slowly, and as quietly as possible, the girls closed the stall door and waited. The herd seemed content at the moment, out of the wind, cozy, dry. But they feared as soon as one of the deer noticed there was no way out….

Bethann came in the barn and assessed the situation with a glance. The girls were all scrunched down and peering in over the tops of the stall boards through the railings. She approached quietly. She would have bet a million dollars that the deer would have fled as soon as the horses started acting up. "You picked a fine time to be silent," she said to Malaki.

Malaki pricked her ears.

Bethann gazed in at the deer and couldn't help but smile. The yearlings had their eyes closed and were all curled up. The four does were eating. The herd filled the stall, but would all have room to lie down and rest. They were safe.

The girls grinned proudly.

"It's time to go," Bethann said, nudging them along.

"Do you think they'll be all right?"

"We'll see," Bethann said. "I'll check on them later."

Little Pixie Dust sneezed.

"Come on. It's time to go home."

~ 31 ~

Mindy spent her time at home, between dinner and going back to check on the deer with Bethann, sitting at the computer researching deer births. She couldn't imagine deer giving birth in this type of weather, yet the doe looked so close. And her aloofness, hanging back by herself, that figured too. According to one site, female deer about to give birth will leave the herd and find a secluded spot where they can be on their own. When they begin labor, they become restless, and stand and sit repeatedly.

"Sit? Deer sit? What, like a dog? Or do they mean down on all fours and not laying flat out?"

When the doe is in the advanced stage of labor, she will remain standing, so that gravity will help the young emerge. In nearly all births, the fawn is born headfirst. After the fawn is born, the mother will lick it dry; do not interfere. The mother will then eat the afterbirth.

"Ick!"

By eating the afterbirth, the female reabsorbs some of the valuable nutrients it contains, and also leaves little trace of blood, which would attract predators. Afterbirth is very, very bloody.

Mindy made a face. "Wow, that's more information than I cared to know."

Fawns have a two out of three chance of surviving their first year. The spots on a fawn's hindquarters and back serve to camouflage it, by breaking up its outline when lying in grasses and brush. A fawn spends the majority of its first few weeks, alone. The dam will only stay with its young the first couple of days after it's born, nursing it every two to three hours. After that, the dam separates herself in order to draw the least amount of attention to her offspring. Do not think the fawn has been abandoned. The fawn knows to lie perfectly still, curled in a ball, and waits patiently for its mother to return several times a day, to nurse.

"Wow, how are they born knowing that?"

After a few days, fawns are able to run. "Hmph," Mindy said. Horses are capable of running the day they are born. Does who did not give birth the year before, will often give birth to twins, and hide the twins in separate areas to ensure at least one survives. The white spots on a fawn's back and hindquarters usually fade at two to three months of age. Weaning begins around six months of age. Although at that stage, weanlings are capable of living alone, they usually stay with their mother until she bears another fawn. If a female fails to conceive, her young will most often stay with her longer.

"Well, that could explain things."

Several does often roam together with their young, forming small herds.

"Yep."

If tragedy befalls one of the dams, the other does will watch over its young.

"Cool."

It is easier to tell a buck's age, because of their neck and brisket. The older they get, the thicker and more pronounced the characteristics become, and also their bellies.

"Like grandpas," Mindy said, chuckling.

The size rack a deer has, since they shed them every year, is an indication of its nutrition level. A young buck can have just as impressive a rack as a veteran, but will not have that solid appearance and girth underneath them. That takes time and perseverance in life, years of supporting rack after rack. When hunting for the older buck....

Mindy switched to another site.

Look at the deer; if it looks young, chances are it is. An older doe will have a slight sway to her back from multiple pregnancies. Some of her young will have lived and some will have died. If you look hard you will be able to see this in her eyes. She will be happy, but she will also be sad. That is the way of the female deer. A doe is never happier than when nursing her young.

"Awe...."

In Shamanism, a deer is said to represent gentleness and love, and epitomize gracefulness, beauty, and peace. They embody sensitivity, keen observation, and innocence. Shamans believe a deer can see through the veils of illusion and are guides through chaos. People can learn from the deer. They can learn how to detect subtle movements and hear things unspoken, and to use their intuition to avoid danger. Deer teach people how to love unconditionally.

"Wow."

In mythology, deer lead heroes to other worlds, and can lure a mere mortal to new adventures, which become opportunities to gain wisdom. When this happens, do not be afraid, but pay heed. As with the deer, when venturing into new territory, one must stay alert and keep your eyes and ears open, for adventure is not always without danger.

Dreaming of deer is a sign of gentleness and healing, and symbolizes the unconscious of the dreamer. If a man dreams of a deer, is it said to signify his feminine side, the Anima, which will lead him into the wilderness. If a woman dreams of a deer, it is a representation of her femininity, in the most primal, instinctive state.

"Hey, Bethann, listen to this." She read the dream paragraph out loud.

"Wonderful." Bethann sighed.

In deer mythology, the beliefs of the people.... Mindy scanned the page. Horns, hooves, fertility, bones and tendons, spilled blood, light, Gods, Goddesses, Cernunnos, Hercules,

Mount Ceryneia, Actaeon, Artemis, immortality and nobility…. To the Pawnee, the deer is a guide to the light of the Sun. The Panche Indians of Columbia believe that human souls pass into the bodies of deer after death and that is why the eating of deer flesh is forbidden to them.

Mindy stared. "Oh my God. Bethann, come here. No, never mind."

"You sure?"

"Uh…."

Bethann appeared at her side. "What?"

Mindy hesitated, then motioned to the screen and sat back. She watched her sister's face as Bethann read the last line. Bethann didn't say anything. She just read it, and then she read it again.

"Do you think Leah Oliver's soul could be in one of the deer?"

"Mindy, please. Don't do this, okay? Move," she said, and sat down, weak in the knees.

"But?"

Bethann motioned for her to be quiet and read the part about the deer dreams.

"What are you looking at?" Mindy asked.

Bethann shrugged.

"Did you have a dream?" Growing up, they were always telling one another their dreams. Mindy thought it was sad that Bethann said she didn't dream anymore. "Was it about our deer?"

"Well, not our deer exactly, just deer in general." Bethann told her about her dream: the flying, the hunters, the deer. And for a moment, the two just looked at one another.

"Wow, this is serious. You never talk in your sleep."

"I know." Bethann shrugged. "But I also had a fever."

"You've had fevers before."

"Good point."

"It's like it's some kind of omen."

"Let's not get carried away."

"Let's look it up." Mindy pulled up another chair and punched in, "dreaming of deer." There were hundreds of listings. "Wow."

A deer in ones dream represents intuition. In Asia, deer are considered conductors of the soul. If you dream of deer, you are perhaps struggling with a decision. A dying deer is a negative omen.

"See, I told you it was an omen."

A dream of witnessing a dying deer might indicate difficult times ahead. Santa Claus uses deer to bring gifts and good tidings. A deer in your dream is a symbol of the gentle and helpful segments of your psyche`.

"I'll take that one," Bethann said.

A deer often appears in a young woman's dreams. It represents the feminine "yin" that has yet to develop into the mother. The deer represents a femininity that tries too hard to please or is too fearful. The feminine aspect deer represent in dreams does not bear authority and power. That comes only from leaving the mother and standing on ones own.

"That doesn't make any sense. Besides, the deer in my dream were bucks and I had nothing to do with them. I was just flying overhead."

Deer are important dream messengers. Deer are vessels of peace. Deer reflect all that is right in the world, and all that is wrong. The entire world can be seen in a deer's eyes.

Bethann shook her head.

"Do you want to know what I think?" Mindy asked.

Bethann hesitated. She wasn't so sure. "What?"

"Now granted, I'm no expert, but...."

Bethann smiled.

"I think you are living in Leah Oliver's shadow. And I think she knows it."

"Mindy...?"

"I'm serious."

"Why would you even say such a thing?"

"I don't know."

~ 32 ~

Bethann made Mindy stay up at the front of the barn while she checked on the deer herself first, just in case. She approached the stall warily...listening. There was no sound whatsoever. She wasn't sure that was a good thing, and could only hope. She was almost afraid to look. She ducked down low so as not to be seen or startle them, and took a deep breath.

Mindy waited impatiently at the other end.

"Please, please, please," Bethann prayed, and straightened up slowly to take a look. Two of the does were standing, along with one of the yearlings. The rest were lying down. All looked well. "They're okay," she said to Mindy.

Her little sister was at the stall front in a flash. "Oh, look at them. They are so cute." She gazed down at Pixie Dust, curled up next to her mom. "Isn't it cool that they're still so close? Oh no, we forgot to water them."

"It hasn't been that long," Bethann said. "I'm sure they've gone longer times than this without water in the wild."

The trick was going to be watering them without scaring them. Fortunately there was an empty bucket hanging in the stall. It was a little dusty, but would have to do. Bethann didn't want to chance opening the door to take it out to wash it. They could slip the end of the hose through the railing and trickle the water in. "Don't make any sudden moves."

One of the standing does had a slight panicky look in her eyes. Malaki didn't like the sound of a hose swishing on, so everyone had developed a way of crimping the hose and running the water slowly until her bucket was full enough to submerge the hose without it making any noise. The method seemed to work for the deer also. The one doe took to walking around the stall, almost stepping on the others. She tried climbing the back wall at one point, and had obviously spent some time earlier doing the same thing. There were fresh scrape marks on the wooden stall boards, some frighteningly high.

"It's okay. It's okay," Bethann said repeatedly, trying to calm and reassure her.

At least the doe wasn't freaking out, though obviously to look at the walls, she or one of the others may have earlier. The doe settled down as soon as Mindy stopped watering and removed the hose. Mindy studied the pregnant one, looking for signs of discomfort while Bethann checked on the horses. They were all either lying down or standing up asleep or half asleep. It was bedtime.

If tonight were the night the pregnant deer decided to give birth, Mindy worried she would not be very happy about not being able to go off on her own.

"Too bad," Bethann said.

"But."

"No. We'll feed them out back in the morning and she can do whatever she likes then."

Benjamin had just gotten home when they returned and as requested, brought a change of clothes for Bethann. They updated him on the latest developments. He had "breaking news" for them too. Jennifer Lynn did a follow up to the deer story and urged people to stay away from Maple Dale so as not to frighten the herd. He'd seen the news while at work. "Didn't you watch it?"

"No. How are the roads?"

"Terrible. It's good you don't have far to go. I am okay coming to your father's house." He'd brought his own shaving cream from home and was feeling like his own man again.

It would be unheard of to have four school-closing snow days in a row, but hope springs eternal. While Bethann and Benjamin had tea in the kitchen, Mindy sat glued to the television. Every other school in the Greater Cleveland area was closed *but* West Geauga. Mindy checked the phone messages. Sometimes Becky's mom knew about the closings sooner, since one of the bus drivers was her best friend.

The only message came from Howard. "Call me," he said, clearing his voice...and then, "Sorry about that."

Mindy laughed. He answered on the first ring. "Hey," he said.

Mindy smiled. Why was talking to him such fun lately?

"I watched the news last night."

"Did you see us?"

"Yes."

"I saw it tonight too."

"What'd it say?"

"Oh, just that because of featuring the deer the previous day, that there were people coming to Maple Dale, and the station was asking them to stop. They said the people were scaring the deer. Is that true?"

"Yes." Mindy told him all about her morning, and then found herself telling him about the rest of her day, even down to what they ate for dinner as if he cared.

He had a hamburger, he said, "Two in fact." He was trying to gain weight.

"Why?"

"Well, not weight actually, just muscle."

"Do you work out?"

"Yes."

"You really aren't a real nerd, are you?"

"No, not actually. Though I don't plan to rob any convenience stores in the near future to prove myself."

Mindy laughed.

"But come to think of it now, I did have a pocket protector once."

Mindy laughed again.

"Who are you talking to?" Bethann asked, on her way to the bathroom. "Is there school?"

"We don't know yet. I'm talking to Howard."

They were both watching their televisions.

"Have you ever ridden a horse before?" Mindy asked.

"No, maybe I'll come ride yours."

"Oh, no. Not Malaki. She's not for a beginner."

"Ooh, low blow."

"I didn't mean that, not exactly at least. She's just temperamental, that's all. She likes my dad, but she really doesn't like other men. Or uh, boys," Mindy said, blushing beet red, though there wasn't a soul in the room with her. "You know what I mean."

"I had a dog like that once," Howard said. "She hated men, guys, males, whatever you want to call them. I was just a boy then, so she liked me."

Mindy giggled. "Point taken. But come on, you *are* only fourteen. That's still considered a boy."

"Actually, I'm fifteen. But whatever."

"I say we let Malaki be the judge."

"Okay, when will you be there next?"

"Tomorrow of course. Call first, though."

"Because...?"

"Because of the pregnant deer. If she's about to give birth, she's going to need solitude. We have a barricade up, so have your mom drop you at the top of the hill."

"How big of a hill? Can I snowboard down?"

"You can try."

"I'll see you then."

"Don't forget to call first."

"Yes, Ma'am," Howard teased.

Mindy blushed again. "Howard?"

"Yes."

"I'm glad you're not my cousin."

"Me, too."

~ 33 ~

West Geauga schools were cancelled the following morning at six-fifteen. The area had gotten only four inches of new snow overnight, but the temperatures had dropped to single digits. Since the county maintenance department used cinders instead of salt for the roads, it was deemed too dangerous for the buses, not to mention too cold for the students waiting at the bus stops.

"Yes! Yes! Yes!" Mindy, Yolanda, and Becky were on the phone together immediately. This week was turning out to be like horse camp, only even better because of the deer. They decided they were going to try to make a homemade pizza today and bake a cake, and divvied up who would bring what and how much. "Who has ice cream?"

Yolanda. She said she'd bring vanilla *and* chocolate.

They were all set.

Bethann was feeling a little better this morning, an improvement over her assessment the day before of: "no better, no worse." She and Mindy ate good breakfasts and off they went. Benjamin was still asleep. That was unlike him. "I think he's getting what I have."

"Oh no."

"I heard him cough a couple of times during the night."

"Give him Vicks."

Yesterday the barn looked like an oasis, today it looked like an ice castle. The siding sparkled in the car's headlights. "Wow!" It looked like someone had dusted it with glitter.

"That is so cool," Mindy said.

Bethann had only seen it one other time like this. "You know, this can only happen under a certain set of weather circumstances. The right temperature, the right amount of snow, which serves as insulation on the ground, combined with the humidity in the air during the day, then dropping to a certain temperature at night and the moisture from within; the horse's body heat, and...."

"You sound like Benjamin," Mindy said, laughing. "Come on, it's magic!"

Bethann laughed. "All right, it's magic." As they got closer, they could see the barn lights on, and then Mrs. Butchling's car. Mindy hadn't felt like making wisecracks about her lately, but did wonder what the woman would have to say about the deer being inside.

"I'll do the talking," Bethann said.

"Why?"

"I don't want a boarder revolt."

"Do you think...?"

"No, but I'll still do the talking anyway."

Mrs. Butchling had already hayed and watered.

"The deer, too?"

Mrs. Butchling was standing just inside the front door, zipping up her jacket and about to leave. "What deer?"

Bethann and Mindy stared.

Mrs. Butchling smiled. "You mean the deer in the stall?"

Bethann and Mindy heaved a sigh of relief.

"They're fine," Mrs. Butchling said.

Mindy hurried down the aisle way to see for herself, approached slowly, so as not to scare them, and gazed in at the herd, all happily eating fresh hay. Bethann and Mrs. Butchling were right behind her. Mindy stared at the pregnant one. Did she look restless? Did she look uncomfortable? No.

"It's fifteen degrees warmer in here than it is outside," Mrs. Butchling said, in her infinite wisdom. "I wouldn't leave them in here long."

"We're going to grain them outside," Bethann said.

"Good."

After she left, Mindy started grumbling. "I don't like her telling us what to do."

Bethann was mixing grain. "She didn't tell us what to do. She just made a good point."

Mindy walked away. "I'll open the back doors."

"If you need help, holler."

Mindy stopped to talk to Malaki, but Malaki ignored her. She was eating her hay and never even raised her head.

"Fine," Mindy said, and walked away from her, too.

The only one in the barn even remotely interested in her at the moment was Dew Drop. For some reason, he wasn't eating his hay. He was standing at the front of his stall and stretched his neck to get her attention.

"What's the matter, big guy? You got a bellyache?"

"Who?" Bethann said, from the feed room.

"Dew Drop."

"Probably not, check his feed tub."

"Uh oh," Mindy said. "He still has some of last night's dinner left."

Bethann thought as much. "I'll check on him, don't worry about it."

"Should I walk him?"

"No."

Bethann had suspected for some time now that Mrs. Butchling had been slipping Dew Drop extra feed. He probably just had a full belly. "I'll check on him, don't worry about it."

"Are you sure?"

"Yes, just go open the back doors, okay?"

Mindy made a face and muttered, "Crabby butt."

"I heard that."

Opening the back doors was even more of a challenge this morning. "Probably you and your barometric pressure," Mindy said. "Oh look, there's some winds aloft."

Bethann laughed.

No matter what Mindy tried, the doors wouldn't budge. She stopped to catch her breath and looked around. All the inside walls had ice sparkles on them as well. It was so pretty.

Dew Drop was still standing at the front of his stall.

"Bethann, you'd better come look at him."

"I'm almost done. I'll be there in a minute. Besides, he's fine."

"How do you know?"

"I just do. What's he doing?"

"Nothing."

"See? He's fine."

Yolanda and Becky arrived, oohed and aahed over the deer, then helped Mindy push and rock the doors. Finally, they opened. By then, Bethann had grained the horses, all but Dew Drop, and mixed the feed for the deer. "All right, here's the plan," she said. They all looked in at the deer. The three yearlings were playing a happy game of push and shove. The pregnant doe was not amused. "Mindy, you take the feed."

"I wanna feed them," Becky said.

"All right, Becky. You take the feed."

They all laughed.

"Becky's going to dump the feed. Mindy, you and Yolanda are going to herd them out. I'm going to stand here and watch and stay out of everyone's way."

They all laughed again.

"Ready?"

"Ready."

As soon as Bethann pulled the stall door open, the yearlings burst forth, tails swishing and climbing on one another. Becky shook the bucket of grain. Mindy and Yolanda waved their arms sending the little ones in the right direction. One doe, then another, and then another and another followed. And in an instant all the deer were outside, eating.

Becky got stuck in the snow, surrounded by them. Mindy and Yolanda each grabbed her by a hand and pulled her free. The girls were all giggling, slipping and sliding, having fun. Then Mindy noticed something: footprints near the side of the barn. Human footprints. Again.

"Maybe it was Mrs. Butchling," Bethann suggested.

"Nope. These are a man's," Mindy said, just like yesterday. "Size elevens would be my guess."

Becky and Yolanda concurred, all three behaving like mystery solving little super sleuths on a difficult case. "Get in here," Bethann said. "Come on, I said now. Let the deer eat."

Next on the girls' agenda, were English muffins. Becky had brought a toaster. "It's an extra. My mom says we can just leave it here." Yolanda brought a stick of butter. Mindy brought jam. They hovered around the toaster in anticipation.

"I love the edges kinda burnt."

"Me, too."

After their snack, they helped Bethann turn the horses out. The barn cleaning crew showed up around ten, finished the stalls quickly, and left for the next farm. By then it was lunchtime. Pizza.

"Do you girls need help?"

"No, we're fine."

Mindy had a box of dough, they mixed it and set it aside to let it rise. They cut up onions and tomatoes, some pepperoni. They had a can of mushrooms, a can of sauce. "Wait a minute, we don't have any cheese."

"Check the fridge," Bethann said.

There was some cheddar way in the back. "Cheddar?"

"Try it."

The girls rated their pizza a 10! "Magnifico!"

They feasted, and then it was time to ride.

"No cantering," Bethann said. "It's too cold. Walk or a slow trot, and that's it." A few degrees colder and she wouldn't have let them ride at all. It was too hard on the horses, not good for their breathing.

To make it fun then, they decided they'd take turns riding one another's horses. They started out on their own, and every ten minutes, stopped and switched. Andy used to be a school horse, so the change of riders didn't bother him a bit. Legs seemed a little concerned. He didn't act up or anything, but certainly wasn't going out of his way to cooperate either. He preferred just Yolanda ride him. And Malaki. Malaki was Malaki. Her Morgan neck gave mixed messages. It was hard for Yolanda and then Becky to figure out if she was tense, about to spook, or just trotting along. Her neck was all muscle and tight, crested. And too much leg had her bucking a little. The girls laughed. When they were done riding and their horses put away, it was time to bake the cake.

"It's snowing again," Mindy announced.

"It never stopped," Bethann said.

"It's snowing harder."

"Are the deer out back?"

"No."

"Howard called. He said to tell you he'll be here in a few minutes."

"Howard?" Becky and Yolanda looked at Mindy. "Why?"

"He's coming to see if Malaki thinks he's a man."

Yolanda and Becky laughed. "Ooh, ooh! I know the answer. Not!"

Mindy told them to shut up. "Both of you!"

"He says he's bringing his friends."

"What?! Which ones? Did he say?"

"No."

"Oh my God."

"Oh my God."

"Oh my God."

"Boys!"

~ 34 ~

The girls threw the cake together and popped it in the oven. Then they hurried and made the frosting, set it aside, and rushed into the ladies room to comb their hair. "They're all going to be nerds," Becky said. "Why should we care?"

"You're the one putting lipstick on," Yolanda said.

Mindy wiped her nose. "They're not nerds. They're snowboarders."

"What?"

"I'm serious," Mindy said. "And just so you know, Howard is not my real cousin."

"So? What's that mean?"

"I don't know," Mindy said. "Nothing. I'm just telling you." The girls bundled up and went outside. "He said he's going to snowboard down the hill."

"Yeah, right."

The girls stood out in front of the barn, in the wind, and in the cold, and in the snow – for what seemed like forever, shivering, and then…. "Look, there they are. Oh my God!"

It was a teenage vision of awesomeness. Wow! And coming their way. These guys were good!

Suddenly the girls didn't mind the cold, and they didn't mind the wind, and the snow was as pretty as ever. Howard was the tallest. They recognized him right away. The other two, they couldn't tell. The one looked familiar. They zigzagged down the hill in all their glory, snowboarding past them, and were headed on a collision course straight for the arena.

"Oh no!"

The boys turned at the last second and crashed into a snow bank, hind-ends first. But apparently that was the intent, or at least a viable way of stopping, since they were all laughing and playing it up, and looking as if they thought they weren't looking cool in the least.

Mindy, Yolanda, and Becky laughed.

The boys unclipped their snowboards from their boots, hoisted them onto their shoulders, and climbed up the hill. "This is Tofer, short for Christopher, and this is Ryan," Howard said.

Christopher was the one that looked familiar; he went to their school. Ryan, they'd never seen before. "I go to Hawken," he said.

"I'm Becky, that's Yolanda, and that's Mindy."

An awkward "so what now" moment followed, whereupon Mindy suggested they go in the barn and see the horses. Malaki didn't like any of the boys. She wouldn't even come to the front of the stall to talk to them. "Didn't I tell you? We're men!" Howard said.

They stopped in front of each horse's stall. Patience was happy to see them; she got lots of attention. Yolanda got to show off Legs, and Becky, Andy.

Peaches was next.

"That's my sister's favorite horse," Tofer said.

"Your sister?"

"She takes lessons here. Her name's Sydney."

"Oh, we know her. She's so cute."

Tofer made a face. "Cute? She's a pain in the butt."

They all laughed. Brothers.

Ryan wanted to know how much everything cost: the tack, the blankets, the horses. "Hey, my dad's a plumbing contractor. Price is the name of the game. How much for this one?"

It was Dew Drop, by far the biggest horse in the barn. "I don't know, probably around fifteen or twenty thousand," Mindy said. "He's for sale if you want to buy him."

"He is?" Yolanda looked at her. Becky, too.

Mindy stared, blushed, and then stammered. She couldn't believe she let that slip. "Just kidding," she said, shaking her head.

"Thanks, anyway," Ryan said, looking up at him and intimidated by Dew Drop's size. "I prefer dirt bikes any day. They don't eat as much and they certainly don't...."

Howard elbowed him before he could finish, and turned to Mindy. "Show us the deer bed."

The girls opened the back doors, easier this time around. The deer were still gone, but there were hoof prints everywhere. "Cool!" the boys said, echoing one another.

"How many deer are there?"

"Seven. Three yearlings and four does."

"No bucks?"

"No."

"Do they all fit in there?" Ryan asked, pointing to the deer bed.

"Yes, but last night...." Yolanda started to say.

Mindy stopped her. "Last night, one of the does had to fight her way in."

"They fight?"

"No, not really. That's not what I meant. I meant...uh.... Did you guys want some cake?"

"Oh no, the cake!" Yolanda took off running.

Not to fear, Bethann had taken it out of the oven. It sat on the counter cooling.

"Oh, thank God."

Mindy, Becky, and the three boys filed in behind her.

"Bethann, this is Tofer, short for Christopher, and this is Ryan. Howard you already know."

Bethann smiled and said hello.

"Tofer's Sydney's brother."

"Our Sydney?"

Mindy nodded.

"My mom's picking us up," Christopher said.

They had just enough time for a piece of cake. It was too warm yet for the icing, but the girls went ahead and frosted it anyway. Some slid off, some stayed on. It was a mess, but good, all melted and warm and with ice cream on the side.

"How much does an arena like this cost?" Ryan asked, licking his fingers.

Mindy shrugged. Priceless, was the word that came to mind. Priceless to her, to Bethann, to Becky and Yolanda, to the other students and boarders, the horses, the cats, the deer...Leah Oliver.

He looked up at the ceiling. "Who put the sprinkler system in?"

"Bethann," Mindy said.

"No, I mean the contractor. What'd he charge?"

Howard smacked him. "Enough, all right?"

They all laughed. The snowplow truck pulled in then; the boys' ride to Alpine Valley. They gathered their snowboards, threw them into the back of the truck, and piled inside. Audra waved and off they went. When the girls sat down for another piece of cake, Mindy became very quiet, thinking. She couldn't believe she'd said that about Dew Drop being for sale. That was supposed to be a secret. And then having to put a price on everything - it reminded her of the stories she'd heard about when Maple Dale was for sale, back before Bethann inherited it. The barns were almost destroyed, and the arenas. The stories were depressing. And today, even Malaki was depressed. What was that all about?

"Where are you going?" Yolanda asked.

"I'm gonna go see Malaki," she said. She'd already brushed her once today, but she was going to go brush her again. And she wasn't going to stop brushing her until Malaki was happy. When she walked into the barn, Malaki was standing at the front of her stall, looking toward the back doors. She didn't even hear her approach, that's how intently she was staring, watching, waiting, listening.

"Is it the deer?" Mindy wondered out loud. Malaki turned toward Mindy when she opened her stall gate, but when Mindy tried to pet her, Malaki stepped away.

Mindy heard pawing at the back doors then. It *was* the deer. She walked down to look and cracked open the doors.

Little Pixie Dust looked in at her and sneezed. "It's not time yet," she told them, counting heads. They were all there. "It's too early. "

The three young ones were shivering.

Mindy had read about how a deer's hair shaft is hollow and puffs up to insulate the animal. The does looked puffed up, the yearlings did not. Maybe if she just let the yearlings in for a while, get them out of the wind. Maybe with it being even colder, they needed to eat more. Mindy looked at the pregnant doe. She seemed restless.

Malaki whinnied. Such a sad whinny.

Mindy didn't know what to do.

She thought about Howard. What did she expect when he came, that he act like a boyfriend? Did he?

Pixie Dust sneezed again. A sad sneeze.

Mindy was sad. They were all sad. She opened the doors and let the yearlings in, and then when the does lined up, she let them in too. The does walked right into "their" stall, the pregnant one leading the way. Mindy pulled the stall door closed behind them, closed the back barn doors, and figured she'd let the youngsters play in the aisle way for awhile.

She laughed, watching them. The other two were getting just as curious as Pixie Dust, just as adventuresome. The three of them peeked under Dew Drop's stall gate, and when he snorted, they took off and ran all the way to the front doors. Mindy realized then, that Malaki still had her stall gate open. All that was keeping her in was her stall chain. Pixie Dust turned around and jogged right up to her. At first Malaki pinned her ears and backed up in her stall. Mindy started toward them, saying "no, no," then, "good girl, good girl." Malaki stretched her neck, sniffing. Little Pixie Dust stood there, swishing her tail. Malaki got closer and closer, and just when Mindy thought she was going to bite her (Mindy almost screamed) Malaki did the strangest thing. She started licking the snow off the little deer's backside, grooming her.

"Oh my God..." Mindy said, and froze.

Her sister and Yolanda and Becky were coming in the front doorway. She motioned for them to be still. They all stood and stared. Malaki was being so gentle. It was hard to believe. And then, she did something even more amazing. She put her head over the little deer's back and pulled it toward her. This was a show of affection usually given by a mare to her foal. She was giving Pixie Dust a "mare's hug."

Pixie Dust stood unafraid. It was as if this was just another doe looking out for her. The other two yearlings stood close by. Then Pixie Dust sneezed, her friends started running and playing, and Pixie Dust chased after them. Malaki watched them, but only for a second or two, and then didn't look so sad anymore. Grabbing her halter off the hook, she started swinging it round and round. It was dinnertime. She wanted to be fed.

~ 35 ~

Benjamin was indeed ill and waiting for them in his car in the driveway when they got to her parents' place. "Why didn't you go in the house?" Bethann asked. "You know where the key is."

He followed them in, hunched over, his hands in his pocket, collar up. "Bed, I need a bed." Bethann fussed over him. She made him tea, she made him soup, she made him more tea. She rubbed his chest with Vicks, she adjusted the humidity in the house, she brought him a piece of cake. She was starting to feel right at home. She loved being this close to the barn. It was less than a half mile away. She loved being on Maple Dale land.

"Honey," she said, adjusting his pillows. "What would you say to us moving here?"

"What? In your father's house?"

"No, just somewhere here in the Maple Dale Community."

"The houses are so big?"

"There are a few smaller ones."

"Are they for sale?"

Bethann shrugged. "There's still some lots available. We could build."

"Is something to think about," he said, yawning.

Bethann kissed him on the forehead. The more tired he became, and obviously sicker, the more Asian he sounded. It was endearing. "Shorter sentences, less energy," he'd said.

"I love you." It had been her idea to move away from the area. She said they needed to put down their own roots. They needed to be their own people, stand on their own two feet. But Maple Dale *was* her roots. It was where she belonged. She knew every inch of it, every tree. It was her home. Why had it taken her four years to realize that?

When Benjamin drifted off to sleep, she went downstairs to check on Mindy. She was at the computer. "Aren't you tired? What are you looking up now?"

"Owls," Mindy said.

Bethann yawned. "Why?"

"Uh...." Mindy hesitated. "Because there's one outside the window."

Bethann turned, hoping she was kidding.

"Listen."

They both heard a faint, "Whoo."

Bethann hesitated. "It's just an owl, Mindy. It's a noise an owl makes. It's just an owl."

"Yeah, but what's he want?"

"Food perhaps," Bethann said, smiling. "Maybe he knows he's the only one on earth you haven't fed yet."

Mindy chuckled. "It says here, that an owl represents the energy of clairvoyance. It is a highly respected animal, and is believed to symbolize the souls of the departed. It could be a bad omen. And, I like this better, the message the owl could be trying to get you to realize, is the power of your own intuition."

Bethann nodded. "*You* are a wise owl, my little sister." She patted Mindy lovingly on the head. "I'm going to bed."

"Good night."

Mindy spent the next hour or so going from one animal website to another, and was glued to one of her favorite sites about Morgan horses when the phone rang. "Hello."

It was Howard. He'd just gotten home from snowboarding.

"Oh my gosh, you were there that long?"

"Yeah, it was awesome. So what are you doing?"

"Um, I'm on the computer."

"And you call me a nerd?"

Mindy chuckled. "I'm only a nerd when it comes to things I want to know."

"Like what?"

"Oh...lots of things."

"Nerd."

Mindy laughed. "What kind of grades do you get?"

"A's."

"Yeah...well, I'm lucky I get C's."

"You don't apply yourself."

"I've heard that before."

"I know."

Mindy laughed again. Of course he knew. After all, he was her tutor "cousin" up until a few days ago, and knew practically everything about her.

"Thanks for showing me your horse," he said.

Mindy smiled. "I'm sorry she wouldn't talk to you."

"I'm not," Howard said. "She deemed me a man!"

Mindy laughed. He really was fun.

"Your friends are nice. Though Ryan was a bit much."

"That's just him."

"Do he and Christopher make straight A's too?"

"Yep. We apply ourselves."

Another laugh. Mindy glanced at the television. She had the sound off, but would check every once in a while for the school closings. West Geauga Schools was still absent from the list.

"So what makes a Morgan a Morgan?"

"Wow, you remembered Malaki was a Morgan?"

"Yeah, she was the only one, right?"

Mindy nodded, as if he could see her - that's how relaxed she was talking to him. "I could give you the whole history of the Morgan, but…."

"How about just the Cliff Notes?"

"Okay. It all started over two hundred years ago with a phenomenal horse named Figure."

"Oh boy." This didn't sound like Cliff Notes to him.

"When his owner Justin Morgan died, Figure's new owner changed the horse's name to Justin Morgan, after the man. That's why they're called Morgans."

"That makes sense."

"Morgans were bred for their stamina, their beauty, and their willingness to please." That she read straight off the site. "Well, I don't know about Malaki and that willingness to please thing. But 'two out of three ain't bad,' I guess."

They both laughed.

"Though actually she can be really sweet sometimes. I don't know why she has those moods. It might have something to with how she was raised."

"Why doesn't she like men?"

"I don't know. I think she probably had a bad experience with one once upon a time."

"Kinda like my mom."

Mindy tried to picture the woman. She really didn't know Howard's mom that well. "I don't know, but whatever happened to Malaki left a huge impression on her. She's never forgotten it. Morgans as a rule are easy to train, but they mature slower. When she was real young, might have been when the problem started. Someone may have expected her to do something she wasn't capable of or ready to do at the time."

"Really?"

"Yeah, that's what Bethann says."

"How long have you had her?"

"Two years. She was really mean when I got her."

"What made you want her?"

"I don't know. We just clicked. And all that bad stuff is behind her now. A good thing about a Morgan maturing later is that as a rule, they live longer. Justin Morgan lived to be thirty-two."

"How long does a horse normally live?"

"It depends on the breed, and obviously the circumstances surrounding his or her life. Justin Morgan would have lived longer, but he got injured out in the pasture and it wasn't treated, so...." Mindy sighed regretfully, as if it happened just yesterday. "Bethann's horse, Persian Sun was twenty-eight when he died. That's old, too. Most live to be around twenty or so."

"Malaki's pretty."

"Thank you."

"So are you."

Mindy fell silent. It was one of the few times in her life she didn't have anything to say.

"So, uh...why are you the only one with a Morgan in the barn?"

"Well." Mindy found her voice again. "A lot of people don't think Morgans make good jumpers. But they're mistaken. I know that for a fact. They make good jumpers and are good for dressage, too."

"Is that what you do? Jumping and dress-age." He pronounced it funny.

"Only enough dressage to supple her. I don't know if that's something I want to do yet. I love the jumping more."

"Okay, what does *to supple her* mean?"

"To get her to bend, to use her back, you know, to stretch. Morgans have a real proud carriage and an upright graceful neck. It's one of their trademark characteristics. It's usually how you can tell them apart from other horses; that uprightness and the crest in their necks, the way they carry themselves. Combine that with dressage, and it's awesome to see."

"Sounds like it."

"Malaki's a classic Morgan from head to toe. She's a prime example. All except for that little glitch with her brain, that is. Do you want to hear what she did today?"

"Yeah, sure."

154

Mindy told him about the "mare hug." How she was afraid Malaki was going to bite the little deer at first, and how gentle she was instead.

"And the deer wasn't afraid?"

"No, that was even weirder."

"Wow."

"I know.

Howard paused. "Are you watching TV?"

"Yes," Mindy said – directing serious attention to the screen in front of her face. "Yes!"

It was the perfect end to a perfect day.

No school tomorrow.

~ 36 ~

The next morning during their phone conversation, the girls decided to be even more creative with lunch, and devised a down-home menu of their favorite things.

"Stuffed peppers."

"You're kidding?"

"They're frozen. We just have to thaw them and pop them in the oven."

"How about mashed potatoes?"

"Sounds good to me."

"Corn?"

"Awesome."

"Brown and Serve rolls?"

"Love 'em."

"And for dessert, how about chocolate mousse."

"Chocolate mousse? Do you think we know how?"

"It's out of a box, how hard can it be?"

It was only three degrees outside, so they knew riding would be out of the question. So were turnouts, even in the indoor arena. "It's just too cold," Bethann said. "The horses are better off in their stalls."

"Bring movies."

"Bring magazines."

"Bring chips."

Benjamin made it downstairs, determined to go to work. Work, work, work. But he never made it out the door. Between the fever, the lightheadedness, and the weakness and the chills, he wasn't going anywhere. "I am so sick," he kept saying.

"Yes, I know." Bethann helped him to the couch.

"How did you make it to work? I am so shamed."

"I had help," Bethann said. "We all need help every now and then."

"I'll go start the car," Mindy said.

"What?!"

"Just kidding." She was anxious to go, anxious to see the deer, anxious to see if there was a new addition. "Do I just turn the key?"

"Don't you dare."

When the phone rang, Mindy grabbed it.

"Mindy? Mindy, it's Mom!"

"Wow, Mom! What time is it there?"

"Eleven at night. Your father wants to talk to you."

"Mindy?"

"Hi, Dad!"

"What's this I hear about you feeding a herd of deer?"

Busted.

"Um…it's only a small herd, Dad. There's only seven of them."

Her dad's exasperated sigh traveled across the Atlantic. "Didn't we have an understanding about this kind of thing?"

"Yes, but they were hungry, Dad. And the one was injured. How did you find out?"

"From Bill. He saw it on the news. He was concerned."

"You don't have to worry. They're okay, Dad. Honest. They're really friendly."

"So I've heard. Put your sister on the phone."

"Don't be mad at her, she had nothing to do with it."

"Mindy…."

"Here she is."

Bethann took the phone and hesitated. "Guess what?" she told her dad, taking the wind right out of his sail. "Benjamin and I are going to build a house in Maple Dale and move home."

"Really? When?"

"What?" she could hear her mother asking.

"She and Benjamin are going to build a house at Maple Dale."

"Really?"

Mindy was just as surprised, all three were thrilled. "Which lot?"

"I'm thinking of the one up on the main hill. It's small, but we don't need a whole lot of yard. We have all of Maple Dale."

"Honey, I couldn't be happier," her father said, getting a little choked up.

Her mom took the phone. "We are so excited. We always hoped you would. But what about Benjamin's allergies?"

"He'll be fine. It's far enough away, I think."

"Oh, Bethann. You have made us so happy. We love you, dear. Tell Benjamin." She handed the phone back to their father.

"Okay, now about your sister..." he said.

"Dad, everything's under control. I just heard the weather's going to change on Sunday and warm up. By Monday, the snow will be melting and they'll probably be gone. And Mindy's okay with that."

"I certainly hope so. I don't want to be there if it all falls apart for her. She breaks my heart when she gets that way."

"I know. Don't worry. Just have fun, okay?"

"Okay." Her dad sighed. "Put her back on the phone."

Mindy had tears in her eyes. Three more days and the deer would be gone? She *wasn't* okay with that. She'd never be okay with that. Bethann shook her head. "Watch what you say, Mindy," she whispered. "This is their time, too. Don't ruin it for them."

Mindy nodded and took a deep breath, wiped her eyes. "Yes, Dad?"

"Damn," her dad said. He could tell she was upset and trying to be brave. "Mindy," his voice cracked. "Listen. I'd change the world for you if I could, but I can't. You have to stop setting yourself up like this. Okay?"

Mindy tried hard not to cry. "Okay."

"We love you."

"I love you, too."

It was a quiet ride to the barn.

Bethann stopped at the top of the hill and pointed to an area of vacant property. "Right there," she told Mindy. "What do you think?"

"I think it would be perfect."

The two of them smiled.

She'd be able to see the barn from home and not one tree would have to fall, because it was all grass and brush. "You're responsible for this, you know," Bethann said.

"Me?"

"Yes. You and your owl, and your talk of dreams, and of Leah. I wish you could have known her. She's everywhere," Bethann said. She drew a deep breath. "This all should have been hers. I guess I thought maybe if I lived here and took over, it would somehow be disrespectful of her. That I would be replacing her."

"I don't think she thinks that."

"Neither do I. Not anymore, at least."

"So what are you saying? Do you think she's still here?"

"She said she'd always be here, that she'd never be far away. And if I needed her…?"

"Do you need her now?"

"I don't know. I have Benjamin. I have you. I have mom and dad, my friends, the students. I don't know." She sighed. "Are you ready?"

Mindy gazed at the barn through the falling snow. It sparkled in the pre-dawn night. "Yes."

Bethann put the car in gear and they took the driveway slowly. It had been plowed already, and there were several other sets of tracks. Mrs. Butchling probably, and….

Bethann's heart dropped. There was a car parked outside the barn, with emergency roof flashers on. Mindy stared. "Oh no...."

"Don't p-panic," Bethann said, driving even slower.

A man got out and stood waiting for them.

He wasn't wearing a gun, but had "official" written all over him.

"He's here for the deer, isn't he," Mindy said. "He's going to take them away, isn't he? I knew it."

"Shhhh...."

Bethann parked and drew a deep breath, trying to calm herself, trying to calm Mindy. "I'll do all the talking. Okay?"

Mindy looked at her with panic and tears in her eyes.

"Promise me, Mindy. I mean it."

"Bethann, don't...."

"Mindy, just go in the barn. All right?"

Mindy nodded.

They both got out of the car.

"Ma'am," the officer said.

Bethann glanced at Mindy as she went inside.

"I'm here about the deer."

Bethann nodded. "What about them?"

"Well, it looks like they haven't been around yet today, but I just want to let you know, that ya'll haven't done them any good domesticating them."

Bethann swallowed hard. Apparently he hadn't been in the barn. That was good.

"I know your sister and her friends had good intentions, but...."

Mindy and Mrs. Butchling stared out through the window at them.

"The problem is you shouldn't have been feeding them. They're wild animals and fending for themselves is a law of nature. The strongest survive. We have too many deer as it is in these parts."

Bethann just listened.

"I've been checking each morning now, this'll be my third morning. I scared them off the one day when they saw me coming. And that's good, don't get me wrong. You don't want them friendly. When they're friendly, they can only cause trouble. They're cute and all and my kids would love them, too. But they're wild animals. For your little sister's sake, I hope they don't come back. You've already broken the law."

"What d-do you m-mean?"

The man took Bethann's stuttering for fear, and made a rather gentlemanly attempt to calm her down, to put her at ease. "The deer bed they built; the one out back. That's sheltering a wild animal. Ma'am, that's against the law. That's not allowed."

"We'll tear it down," Bethann said. "We don't want any trouble."

"I understand." He tipped his hat to her and got in his car. "The problem is those seven deer aren't afraid of people anymore. They're going to be a nuisance. I'm sorry, but we can't have that."

"What are you saying?"

"I'm saying, if we get a complaint - just one, and we will, we're going to have to come take care of them. I'm sorry."

~ 37 ~

Bethann waited until the man's car forged the hill and pulled out onto the highway below, before entering the barn. "Who was that?" Mindy asked. "What did he want?"

"Are the deer inside?"

Mindy and Mrs. Butchling nodded.

"Are they okay? What about the pregnant one?"

"They're fine. She's fine. No baby yet."

Mrs. Butchling had already hayed and watered the horses and deer.

Bethann sat herself down on the nearest stool, trying to decide what to say, what to do. "He's a county official. He said we can't feed the deer anymore."

Mindy gasped. "What? Why? Can't we feed them till Monday?"

"He says no. He says it's illegal."

"Who cares?" Mindy said. "I don't care! What are they going to do, arrest me?"

"Yes," Bethann said, looking up at her. "You, me, Mrs. Butchling, Yolanda, Becky...."

"Oh really?" Mrs. Butchling got a defiant look on her face. "Oh, like that's going to bring me to my knees. I'm losing my husband; he doesn't even know my name. I have to sell my horse. I'm probably going to end up losing my house; my home...and they're going to arrest me for feeding some poor defenseless deer? Tell them I said to bring it on! At least I'll have a frigging place to sleep."

Mindy crossed her arms over her chest and nodded in support. "Yeah, bring it on!"

Bethann shook her head and had to smile. Who wouldn't, with the two of them taking such a stand? "I can see it all now. Dad, c-could you come bail me and Mindy and Mrs. Butchling out of jail? (But I'm in Europe, honey.) That's okay, we'll wait."

The three of them laughed nervous giddy laughs.

"What are we going to do?" Mindy asked.

"I don't know." Bethann stood and dusted off her backside. "Right now I'm going to grain."

Mrs. Butchling had to leave for work. "Call me," she said.

Mindy mixed the pellets and oats for the deer.

"Feed them inside," Bethann told her.

"You sure?"

"Yes. It's uh, too cold, and the d-door probably won't budge so...."

"Are you all right?" Mindy asked, hesitating.

Bethann nodded. "I just need to think. Go on."

When all the animals had been grained, Mindy hauled the groceries out of the car and into the kitchen. Bethann went into her office. Becky and Yolanda arrived a few minutes later. Bethann greeted them and then closed her door. Mindy told them the news.

"You're kidding?"

Mindy shook her head.

"That sucks!"

"I know."

"What are we going to do?"

"I don't know. Bethann's thinking."

The three of them sat looking at one another. When the phone rang, they all jumped.

Bethann answered it in the office. When she glanced up, all three girls were staring in at her. "It's okay," she said, motioning. It was one of the boarders. Bethann talked them into not coming out today. "It's too cold," she said, which was true. But she was also buying time until she could decide what to do about the deer. She looked through the side window at the outdoor thermometer, two degrees.

She phoned Benjamin. She'd left him the phone within reach. "Uh huh," he said, answering. That was encouraging. One, that he'd answered, and two, his usual greeting.

"I just want to let you know what's going on," she said, and told him the story.

"Not good," Benjamin replied.

"There's no way I can keep the boarders away until the weather breaks. I can keep them away today; I'm going to call them all as soon as I hang up with you. But even so, we can't turn the deer loose. It's like the guy said, they're not afraid of people anymore."

Benjamin sighed, listening. "Can you take them somewhere?"

"What do you mean?"

"Like to a zoo or something?"

"Uh...I don't know. I don't even know if the zoo's open. Or if I contact them, what trouble that might cause."

"I hear you. I'll try to find out," he said, standing and almost tipping over. "Where is closest computer?"

"In the den? Are you sure you're okay?"

Benjamin looked around the room, all four or five fuzzy-wavy versions of it. "I'll shoot for the middle," he said. "I am on the job."

Bethann thanked him, hung up, and phoned all the boarders and students next. When that was done, she sat back and took a deep breath. The girls were cooking something already; she could smell it. It smelled really good. She went to investigate.

It wasn't even eleven o'clock yet and they'd cooked a full-course meal. They'd even set the table. A slightly dusty centerpiece adorned the middle of the table. Each paper plate place setting had two plastic forks on one side and a plastic knife and spoon on the other with a napkin folded neatly underneath. Yolanda pulled a chair out at the head of the table for Bethann to sit down.

"Who else is coming?" Bethann asked, looking at the chair to her right.

"Now don't get mad," Mindy said. Yolanda and Becky nodded. "But that's for Leah Oliver, in the event she *is* here."

Bethann paused to take it all in. They'd put a lot of thought into this. "I don't want to encourage you girls."

"You're not," Yolanda said. "We're encouraging you."

Bethann smiled. "Well, I don't know about Leah, but I'm very hungry, so...." The girls served the food. They all sat down, and Becky said grace.

"Amen."

Bethann looked at them proudly. These girls weren't lawbreakers. They weren't even troublemakers. They were just three young women who would try and feed the world if they could. "This is an honor," Bethann said. "Thank you. Everything looks delicious." She was going to enjoy the meal. She was going to enjoy the moment. She was going to enjoy their company. And if Leah were at her side, she was going to enjoy her presence, too. Because who knew what the rest of the day would bring?

~ 38 ~

Benjamin phoned a little over an hour later. The news was not encouraging. "There is no one of authority to talk to at the zoo today. Everyone is busy taking care of the animals. They said call Monday. Also...." He rustled a piece of paper, his notes, Bethann surmised. Benjamin wrote down everything. "Deer don't transport well. You must be careful."

"I didn't say I was going to transport them."

"What else can you do, lasso like rodeo cowboy and drag them away?"

He sounded cranky, Bethann had to laugh.

"They will become frantic in confinement."

"These deer are used to confinement."

"You will have to protect the little ones from the adults."

"It doesn't matter. It's illegal to transport them."

"Yes, it says that, too. You would have to have a license of some kind. You must be a propagator."

"A propagator?"

"I have a list."

"Are there any in Ohio?"

"They are all in Ohio. I have an Ohio list."

Bethann smiled. He was so good. "Can you fax it to me?"

"Where is fax?"

"In my dad's office."

Silence.

"It's okay; he won't care."

Silence, still.

"I'd come home, but I don't want to leave. If this guy would decide to come back...."

"I am dizzy."

Bethann hesitated. "Do you w-want me to come home?"

"No. I just need to catch hold of my breath."

Bethann glanced at the girls. They were letting her know they were going to the barn. She nodded. "Are you sure you're all right?" she asked Benjamin.

"Yes. I go now."

Bethann chuckled. He could be so dramatic. "Thank you. I love you." She hung up the phone and waited. Waited, and waited, and waited. Fifteen minutes passed. She was just about to phone him back, when the fax came through. "Thank heaven."

Who would ever think there would be this many propagators in Ohio? She scanned down the list of names and locations, first page, second page. "Winnie," she said, and felt a chill. She knew a Winnie once; she used to ride at Maple Dale. What would be the odds? She glanced around the room. She could almost see Winnie here, sitting on the chair, standing, drinking soda, talking about riding. And for a moment, a brief second, she could almost see Leah, shaking her head and smiling at them.

She picked up the phone and called Lucy G. for the second time today. "Do you remember Winnie from years ago?"

"Yes, why?"

"Um... do you know if she got married?" The propagator Winnie had a different last name.

"I think so. The guy had a really odd name."

"Porkolowski?"

"Yes, that's it! Why?"

"I don't know. I just ran across it, and...."

"She was a lot of fun, remember? Remember how we used to call her Winnie Schminny?"

Bethann chuckled. "Cause she was so skinny."

"Yes."

"Maybe when the weather breaks, we should look her up and go have lunch or something."

"That sounds like fun. Let me know."

Bethann hung up and stared at Winnie Porkolowski's address and phone number. She imagined the phone conversation. "Hi, Winnie. It's Bethann. Remember me from Maple Dale? Listen, could you tell me what I can do to become a propagator in a day?"

She sat back, remembering the day she and Lucy and Winnie went with Leah to the Coliseum south of Cleveland to see the Lipizzaners. A whole busload of them went, and it was a lot of fun. She looked out into the arena, imagining a Lipizzaner under saddle, a magnificent animal awaiting her. She sighed. Accomplished as she was, she couldn't imagine riding one. What she really wanted to ride, was a horse like Persian Sun.

When the fax machine clicked on again, the noise startled her. "Thought you might want to read this," Benjamin had written across the top. It was an article on Whitetail Deer, Ohio's state animal, and the disastrous effects of their over-population in one small Ohio town.

Bethann hadn't realized the Whitetail Deer was Ohio's state animal. The entire article was an eye opener. She read each word, each line with trepidation. It was a perfect little town, neatly painted clapboard houses with beautifully landscaped lawns and gardens, a local horticulturist club, four churches, no bars. It was heaven on earth. An evening in this town was spent on front porches; lazily watching what little traffic there was, go by. The residents fed the birds, they fed the squirrels. They fed the *resident* Whitetail buck. That TV program "Northern Exposure" had its Bull Moose. Rainbow Valley, so named for its abundance of sunshine and rain three seasons out of the year, had its lone Whitetail buck.

One harsh winter, two more Whitetail Deer stumbled onto the streets, two yearling does. They were tired. They were weary. They were hungry. And seemingly in the blink of an eye, they were pregnant. The townsfolk took care of them and awaited their fawns' arrival. One gave birth to twins, the other, triplets. They were tame, they were gentle. They adored being fed by hand. They feared no one; no one feared them. That's where the fairy tale ended. The deer ate and ate and ate. And soon, others came to feast, and then more and more. A town meeting was called. Something had to be done about the expanding herd. The deer were ruining lawns, devouring flowers and shrubs. They were urinating and defecating on the sidewalks and in the streets. They were causing car accidents.

"I have no lawn," an angry resident cried. "Just paw paws," which was a plant not even deer liked.

"I haven't seen a chipmunk in weeks," said another.

"Or a butterfly."

"Or a rabbit."

"I can't remember the last time I saw an owl."

"What happened to the hawks and the falcon?"

"My vegetable garden is ruined."

"My trees have no bark."

Common plants and shrubs that once grew abundant in the area were scarce. The woodland asters, goldenrods and rarer species such as trillium and fringed gentian had all but vanished. Sumacs, stripped of their bark by the hungry deer, were rapidly disappearing. Jewelweed, an important food for small birds and mammals, were virtually gone. Tree seedlings had been eaten so intensely that forest regeneration had ground to a halt. Ground-nesting birds had become a thing of the past. Rainbow Valley was fast becoming a barren wasteland.

"It's the deer or us. There's not enough room for both."

"How did this happen? What should we have done?"

"More importantly, what should we do now?"

Whitetail Deer in general have flourished because of lack of predators. Needless to say, there were no wolves or mountain lions in or near Rainbow Valley, no coyote either.

"I say we bring in sharpshooters."

Deer culling was nothing new. Park managers all over the country have had to resort to deer culling at one point or another. What had recently been considered viable alternative solutions, such as fencing, relocation, and birth control, were proving costly and dangerous, and in most cases, ineffective.

"I say let nature take its course. Whenever people try to control things, we make matters worse."

Naturalist sentiment aside, culling had not proven to be all that successful either. To appease public opinion, in some areas and in some states, only the bucks were culled. The following year, the ratio of male to female deer born, was an astounding three to one. Plus, more does gave birth to twins and triplets than the previous years. Survival of a species? The scientific jury is still out.

The question then to consider, should only the does be culled? The answer is no, according to some experts. They believe correct culling should be across the board; bucks, does, the young, the old, and yes, even the newborn fawn. This option curdles the blood of even the staunchest of hunters.

There are some who blame global warming for the increase of deer. The less harsh the winters, the more vegetation the deer can access, then the more survive. If food is not plentiful, as in the cyclic harsh winters of old, the doe will not settle and she will not bear young. Advocates of this theory believe there is a direct correlation between the increase of deer and ozone depletion. Others say that is hogwash, that deer have become a problem over the years, because man has ceased to be the hunter/gatherer. Get out your guns.

Could clear-cutting acres of brush and sowing them with oats grown specifically for the deer, be the answer? Feed them to keep them away? Perhaps. But it would be at the expense of the rabbit, the moles, the squirrel, and the chipmunk, among others. Feeding the deer in the long run, only adds to the problem. The dinosaur is extinct. To some, that is sad. And to others, merely practical. We no more need a dinosaur in our lives today, than a herd of hungry deer in our backyards. Drop them in their tracks.

Bethann looked up when the girls returned and folded the fax. There was only a paragraph or two left. She vowed to read the rest later; she wanted a happy ending. "Are the deer okay?"

The girls nodded.

"We think the pregnant one is about to give birth," Mindy said.

"We're leaving her alone."

"We made a bed for her in the blanket room."

"She walked right in."

"It was as if she knew we were trying to help her."

"She said thank you."

"We named her Belle."

~ 39 ~

Bethann phoned Winnie Porkolowski and waited, behind closed doors, for her to answer. The girls were watching a video; she was making them stay out of the barn.

"Hello."

"Is this Winnie?"

"Yes."

"Winnie, this is Bethann Sim, um…formerly Bethann Morrison."

"Hey! How the hell are you?"

"Fine! How about you?"

"Great! Do you have any kids?"

"No, not yet. What about you?"

"Two. They're both brats, but ya gotta love 'em!"

Bethann laughed.

"You're still at Maple Dale, I hear."

"Really? I mean, yes I am. But how…?"

"I saw you on the news. How are the deer?"

"Well, that's kind of why I'm calling you."

"Let me guess."

Bethann told her the whole story. She was initially only going to tell her part of it, but Winnie was a sympathetic ear and asked all the right questions. "I don't know what to do," Bethann said.

"Hold on a minute. Brian, I said sit down right now. Kids! Oh, is this one a handful. I'm sorry, you were saying."

Bethann hesitated. "So what's this about you being a p-propagator?"

"Oh that. I harvest injured falcons."

"Wow!" Bethann made sure to sound excited for her, but her heart was dropping. Falcon and deer were worlds apart. "How'd you get into that?"

"Oh, sort of like you. I came across one that was injured, got in trouble for saving him, and like they say, the rest is history. I've had five of them over the last couple of years. They're fascinating."

"I'll bet. So what do you think I should do?"

"I don't know. Let me see what I can find out. Brian, now quit! I mean it!"

Bethann paused.

"I'll call you. Give me your number."

Bethann gave her all three, thanked her, and hung up, depressed. So much for that.

It was still snowing. She stared out the window. It was two o'clock. If it wasn't for all the snow and this wasn't real life - if this were only a fairy tale or a dream she'd load the deer up and drive south to where there was no snow. She'd find a place where no one was around so she could turn them loose. They'd all live happily ever after. And if she didn't feel like making the drive back, she'd just lift herself up into the sky and fly home.

Mindy knocked on the door. "What are you smiling about?"

"Nothing," Bethann said. "You."

"Me?"

"Yeah, you got me dreaming again. Who cares if I'm wide awake?"

Mindy chuckled. "Can we go back out and check on her?"

"No." Bethann motioned for her to go find something else to do.

Mindy stuck her tongue out at her and left. The three girls decided to play cards. There was an ancient deck in the top drawer in the kitchen, bound with an old dry-rotted rubber band, which broke when they removed it. All three looked up at Bethann when she came out of the office, putting on her jacket and gloves.

"I'll be right back. No, don't any of you follow me."

"Hmph," Becky said, when she'd gone. "She really is aging before our very eyes."

The three of them laughed.

"It's a shame these aren't tarot cards."

"They're even better," Mindy said. "They're Leah Oliver's."

"You're kidding."

"Maybe."

Becky and Yolanda stared down at their poker hands. "How long has she been dead?"

"Fifteen years."

The cards certainly looked that old, maybe even older. Mindy took their cards, gathered up the rest, and shuffled the deck. "First one to draw a queen will be the first one to marry."

"Who cares about marriage? How about a first date?" Yolanda said.

"The number card will tell you how many children you're going to have."

"Oh great," Becky said, when she got hers. "I'm having five red ones."

"Red and yellow, black and white," they sang in unison. "They are precious in his sight, Jesus loves the little children of the world!" They laughed, that familiar Sunday School hymn popped into their head spontaneously/simultaneously.

"I'd rather just have horses and deer."

"Me, too."

According to the cards, Yolanda was going to have ten children. "Ten?!"

Mindy was going to have two. "I'll take a boy and a girl." She shuffled the deck again. "The next number card will tell us how many boyfriends we'll have before we meet the one we're going to marry."

Eight for Yolanda. "Cool!" Six for Becky. Nine for Mindy. Bethann returned and went straight into her office. The three girls got up and followed her.

"Well?"

"She's fine, just lying down."

"Does she look uncomfortable?"

"No."

"So what's going on?" Mindy asked. "What's gonna happen?"

"I'm not sure," Bethann said. "I'm working on it. Go away."

All the girls frowned, leaving. Bethann motioned for them to close the door, and they went back to playing cards. Mindy didn't know it, but her dad had sat at that same table some fifteen years ago playing gin rummy with Bill Forbes during another crisis, with the same deck of cards. There were no horses here then, no students. In fact, Maple Dale was scheduled for demolition at the time and it was just the two men, keeping guard.

Bethann answered the phone when it rang, hoping it would be Winnie calling back with information, possible solutions, prayer, anything. It was Jennifer Lynn. "I'm sorry," she said. "I guess I got you all in trouble."

Bethann chose her words carefully, becoming paranoid all of a sudden. "Trouble? What do you mean?"

"I guess feeding and housing the deer is illegal. We didn't know that."

Bethann ventured a comment. "Neither did we."

"We ran another segment on it at noon, discouraging others from doing the same thing."

"Okay," Bethann said, for lack of something better to say.

"I'm sorry. If there's anything I can do, just let me know."

Bethann thanked her and hung up the phone, the words of an old John Denver song playing in her mind. "Take me home, country roads, to the place...I belong, West Virginia...."

The phone rang again. "Hello."

"Bethann, it's Mom."

Bethann slumped in her chair. Oh gees, what now?

"Your dad wants to speak to you."

Bethann laughed in spite of herself. Why couldn't he ever just dial the phone himself?

"Bethann?"

"Before you say a word...." Bethann scrambled to come up with a diversion, fast. "I'm so glad you called. It's about uh...." She looked out the window. "It's about Mrs. Butchling. She had to put her husband in a n-nursing home." "Oh, that's too bad. The Alzheimer's?" "Yes. She thinks she's going to lose her house and she's going to have to sell Dew Drop." "What kind of insurance does she have?" "I don't know. Why?" "Sounds like someone's doing a number on her with some scare tactics. Tell her not to do anything till I get back. Tell her to gather up everything, hospitalization, major medical, life insurance. I'll need to see it all. Now about your sister." "Dad, it's all under control. I promise. It's like I told you earlier." "Yes, well I heard from Bill again and happen to know otherwise. This is three days in a row now that you girls have made the news." "Is Mindy okay?" her mother asked, clutching his arm. "Your mother wants to know if Mindy's okay?" "Yes, why wouldn't she be?" "Didn't they come and get the deer?" "No...um, they uh...weren't outside, um, out back anymore, so...." "Good, we'll be home tomorrow." "Dad, don't...." "We'll let you know when our flight will be in." "No!" Bethann said. "Put mom on the phone. Mom, if you two come home, I will never forgive you. Do you hear me, never! I am a grown up and you two have got to let me handle this! This isn't fair. Don't do this! Let me talk to Dad. Dad! I'm serious. I mean it. Stay where you are and have fun for God's sake! This is all under control. Okay?!" Her father hesitated. "Okay." "Good. Thank you. Thank you about Mrs. Butchling, too. I'll let her know. Good-bye." "We're going to call you tomorrow." "Fine."

"We'll talk to you then."

She hung up the phone and sat back with a new resolve. She was going to give providence and fate just fifteen more minutes, and after that, take matters into her own hands. She stared at the folded fax. Now seemed as good a time as any to read the last two paragraphs.

If culling the herd is not the answer, then the same can be said for feeding the deer. At the start of rutting season, several factors dictate the amount of fawns that will be born the coming year. If deer are hungry, not starving, but not getting as much food as they should, then the sex drive of the bucks will decline and the undernourished does will not ovulate. There would be fewer reproductions. Plus there would be a normal die-off due to the lack of food.

That made sense to Bethann. Probably why only one of the four does was pregnant. Mother Nature's way.

In theory, within a few years the deer population would stabilize and adjust to the capacity of a territory. If there were less space and less food, there would be less deer. The species has evolved because of innate survival mechanisms, assumptions that have been true for millions of years. The question would be, can modern man stand by and trust this species to continue evolving. The residents of Rainbow Valley are struggling with this decision.

The phone rang. "Yes?"

"Hey, it's Winnie. I think I have something for you."

Bethann's fifteen-minute wait wasn't even up yet.

"There's this woman that's going to call you. Her name is Susan Nelson. She's a bit eccentric, but has a heart of gold. When she phones you, follow her lead. Don't ask any questions, just go along. She might be able to help you out."

"Okay. But what's she going to tell me?"

"I don't know. She doesn't have much use for people, so watch what you say."

Bethann hung up the phone and stared at the receiver. Here she was, waiting again, and with the clock ticking away. If they turned the deer loose, the pregnant doe was going to give birth in a blizzard. If they turned the deer loose, they'd be standing at the back door in the morning, and be shot. If they turned the deer loose, seven, soon to be eight, of God's most gentle creatures, will have lost their lives for nothing. Ring, phone, ring.

~ 40 ~

When it came time to feed, Bethann told the girls to go on ahead, but to just hay and water. She'd be there in a few minutes to grain. She sat with her elbows on the desk and her head in her hands. She was nearing the "end of her rope," as the saying goes. It was still snowing; in fact it was snowing even harder now. She was still waiting to hear from this Susan Nelson. She didn't know what to do. She worried she might be waiting for nothing. She needed to come up with a plan of her own.

"Bethann."

She looked up from her desk. "Yes," she said.

No one was there.

I'm exhausted, she thought, and shrugged it off, probably just getting carried away with this daydreaming thing. After all, I did have my eyes closed. Maybe I dozed off. She looked around the room.

No sign of life, present *or* past.

She saw a flash of light outside the window and looked into the falling snow. She stared harder. "Leah?" She rubbed the windowpane, trying to see clearer, the blowing snow…the image….

Her attention was suddenly diverted beyond; headlights approaching the barn. She grabbed her jacket and gloves, and threw them on as she hurried out the door. It was the same car from this morning, same man.

"Hello," she said, when he got out of his car.

"Ma'am." He tipped his hat.

"What can I do for you?"

"I'm just making rounds," he said, and started up the hill to behind the barn.

Bethann was right with him, slow going in the almost two feet of heavy snow. "We haven't s-seen them out back all day."

The man stopped at the top of the hill to get his second wind, and then trudged down below. The deer bed was covered in snow, no deer tracks anywhere.

Bethann's heart beat a hundred miles an hour.

"Well, it's a good thing ya'll stopped feeding them," he said. And that's all he said. His jaw was fast freezing. He motioned to the back doors. It certainly would make more sense to go back through the barn.

"The doors are frozen," Bethann said.

He pulled on one, and motioned for her to step back. Another tug, and then another.

Bethann held her breath.

He kicked the bottom of the one hard with the back of his heel. Kicking it that hard, sooner or later it was going to open.

"I'm sorry," Bethann said. "But I'm freezing." She started up the hill, didn't dare glance over her shoulder, and could only hope....

He gave up his quest and cimbed the hill behind her. "I've never seen this much snow," he said, huffing and puffing. "Least not this late in the year."

Bethann stopped at his car, hugging her sides and shivering. "You drive careful," she said.

The man nodded and opened his car door. A rifle lay across the passenger seat. "You too, Ma'am," he said. But Bethann couldn't hear him. She was already practically to the observation room. She slipped at one point, and could have prevented herself from falling, but didn't. She fell, got up and waved, and waved again from the door, anything to divert his attention away from the barn. What if he asked to take a look inside? But why would he? What if one of the girls opened the door? Were the doors locked? What if...?

The man got in his car and started to pull away. Bethann watched from behind the wallboard. He started sliding, sliding, and sliding, and slid to a stop. "Oh dear God, no..." Bethann muttered.

He backed back down and started up again.

"Oh, please..." she prayed. "Please, please, please...."

He got just a little further than the first time and started sliding again. He wasn't going anywhere, not without help. She saw herself having to get the tractor out of the barn, saw herself turning and seeing the man in the aisle way, saw herself trying to stop him from approaching the deer...could he hear them, could he smell their deer scent?

She stared. The man's car began sliding sideways again, his engine building to a roar. He didn't back down the hill, he just sat spinning and spinning, and all of a sudden his car started creeping up the hill. "Go," Bethann said. "Go." He spun and he slid, advancing little by little, and at the top of the hill, disappeared. She ran to the other window, waiting to see his headlights fan out onto the highway. "Yes," she said. "Thank you! Thank you!"

She bowed her head and drew a deep breath through lungs that hurt, and went to check on the girls. When she opened the door, they were all three standing just inside waiting for her. "Oh my God, we thought he was going to get the back door open. We kept pushing against it! We were so afraid!" They were all three in tears. "Malaki warned us! Didn't you, girl?" Mindy said, rushing over and hugging her.

Malaki nodded her head up and down, definitely agitated and on-the-muscle about something. "She kept whinnying and whinnying! Didn't you hear her?"

"No," Bethann said.

The girls wiped their eyes and dragged Bethann down the aisle way to Belle's stall. The doe lay flat out, her breath coming in short little wisps.

"She's getting closer," Mindy said.

From the other end of the barn, Malaki whinnied. The cry echoed throughout. She was obviously still upset about the man being there, and probably why she'd been so sullen the last couple of mornings. Had he entered the barn those two days? Would he be back in the morning? It was just a matter of time before he....

Belle raised her head, looked at her side, and then laid her head back down. "Let's leave her alone," Bethann said, fighting back tears. "Come on."

She quickly mixed the grain, did the supplements and meds and they fed. Then she herded the girls back to the observation room. Witnessing the deer giving birth would be a wonderful experience for the girls, witnessing the deer give birth with complications would not. Since there was no way of knowing and neither of them was qualified or even knowledgeable enough to assist if a problem did arise, she felt it best to leave this entirely up to Mother Nature.

When the girls continued balking about having to stay inside, she had them read the faxed article that Benjamin had sent. It wasn't about birth, but it was definitely about "human interference." It silenced them. Bethann sat down at her desk, exhausted, and glanced at the phone. "Oh no." There was a message on the answering machine. "Please be from Benjamin."

It was from Susan Nelson. She sounded ancient. "Hello! This is Susan. Is anyone there?" There was noise in the background. "Damn, I don't have time for this!" she said, and hung up. The sound of the answering machine hum in the wake of her voice had every bit the effect of a heart monitor flat lining…. No message, no phone number, no hope.

Bethann sat back and burst into tears. She couldn't help herself. She couldn't hold it back, she couldn't stop, she just kept crying. When the girls appeared at her side, she told them why, and they all started crying too.

"No!" Mindy kept saying. "No!"

Yolanda grabbed the phone, punched in some numbers, and said. "I have it! I have her number!"

Bethann wiped her eyes, looking up at her.

"Automatic call back."

"We have that?"

"Yes." Yolanda dialed the number and handed her the phone. It rang twice.

"Hello!" Sharon Nelson said, same ancient voice, same agitation. "Who is this?"

"Bethann Sim." Bethann wiped her eyes. "You just phoned?"

"Oh yeah." The woman cleared her throat. "I can hardly hear you. I'm in the barn. I called you about my deer."

Her deer...? Bethann hesitated, for one – taken aback. And two, Winnie said to watch what she said and to follow the woman's lead.

"Hold on. Here you go, you little shit," the old woman said.

Bethann smiled, nodding to the girls, her tears starting to dry up. She could hear what sounded like a lamb, baaing.

"No, no, no. Get out of the way. Go," she said, and then, "How soon can you get them here?"

Bethann hesitated, was she talking to her?

"Hello?"

"Yes. I'm here."

"I said how soon can you get them here?"

"Um...." Bethann looked out the window. "Where are you?"

"Piedmont. Do you know where that is?"

"Uh, vaguely." Not really.

"My property is on both sides of the state."

What states, Bethann wondered? Did she dare ask? Please have one of them be Ohio.

The woman gave her the address. "If I'm not in the barn, come to the house. Any problems along the way, give them my name. The deer belong to me; you're just returning them. I don't know how they got so far away. Okay? I've gotta go now. "

"Wait!"

Silence.... Bethann feared she'd hung up, but then heard an exasperated sigh, and swallowed hard. "One of the does is about to give birth."

"I know."

"No, I mean any minute now."

"If she does, don't touch them."

"Them?"

"Them, it, Jesus! However many, don't touch them!" she barked. Bethann heard her talking to someone else, another person perhaps, more than likely an animal, judging from her happier tone of voice. Then the line went dead. She'd hung up.

Bethann hesitated. Should she call her back; a million questions ran through her mind? At the top of the list, was the illegal transporting of wildlife issue.

The girls waited anxiously for her to say something, anything. She needed to talk to Benjamin, she needed a map. She needed a weather report. She needed strength. She could drive her truck and trailer in her sleep, but in a driving snowstorm, a blizzard? That concerned her.

"Sit down," she told the girls.

They dropped to the floor as one. Their combined action caused everyone to laugh, even Bethann. "Get up." She motioned to the couch, and then the phone rang.

"For Christ sake, I forgot to tell you," Susan Nelson said without so much as a hello. "Do you have a CB?"

"No, I have a cell phone."

"That's not going to do you any good. How would you know anybody's number down here?"

Good point.

"My handle is 'Sassy Susie.'"

No kidding, Bethann thought.

"Channel 14."

Click.

~ 41 ~

Benjamin was not happy. Piedmont was two hours away on a good day and nothing more than a tiny dot on the map some thirty miles off a main highway. "You don't even know this woman. This is crazy."

Bethann had to agree, though not out loud. "Did you get a weather report?"

"Yes, snow, snow, and more snow."

"Down there, too?"

"Yes, everywhere in the state." He coughed. "This is crazy," he repeated. Piedmont, on the Ohio side, butted up to a little town called "Masonville," that was just across the state line into West Virginia. "It's too far."

"I didn't say I was going."

Mindy, Becky, and Yolanda stared, aghast.

"I said I was just thinking about it. That's why I'm talking to you."

Benjamin fell silent.

"Let me call you back. I want to go check on the doe."

The girls followed her. "Stay put," she told them, just inside the barn. She crept down the aisle way slowly. Malaki nickered to her. "Shhh...." She stopped to appease her, patted her on the head, and walked on. Every horse watched her every move. Bethann was a believer in the true essence of nature. She was encouraged that the horses knew something was taking place. They obviously sensed it, and were watching over the deer, even if they couldn't see her. In a pasture, other mares will circle a mare about to foal, to protect her, to support her. And even some geldings. Maybe in their own way, the horses in the barn were doing the same thing. They all stood looking down the aisle way, watching and waiting.

Bethann tiptoed to the stall and looked in at Belle. She'd already had one fawn and was on her feet, giving birth to another. Bethann motioned for the girls to wait, but then on second thought, motioned for them to come, quietly. The girls deserved to be a part of this. The deer belonged to them, to the world.

The second fawn lay next to the first, all wet and dazed as the girls peered in, their hands to their faces in awe. Belle turned and started nuzzling the fawns. They looked surprised. The one kept fluttering its ears in such a cute little way. And the other one kept trying to bury its head.

"I'll bet he's a boy," Mindy whispered.

Belle raised her eyes and looked at the four of them. She didn't look at them long, she had things to do, her young to care for. But for a brief moment, as she gazed from one to the next, it was as if they were being blessed. Thank you, she appeared to be saying. Thank you.

Bethann gave them all a hug. "Congratulations."

"You, too. We couldn't have done it without you." They were all in tears.

Bethann laughed softly. "Well, that may be true, but...." There was still a lot left to do, for her as well as the doe.

"She needs to eat her afterbirth," Mindy said, making a face.

"How about we leave her alone to do that?"

They all walked over to check on the other deer. The does were standing, facing the front of the stall and listening. Pixie Dust and the other two yearlings were lying down; sound asleep. Their time to give birth and fret and worry over their sisters and mothers and cousins and friends would come soon enough. Bethann went back to the office and phoned Benjamin again. "We now have nine deer," she told him.

He sighed.

"Benjamin...?" She had to go; she had to take them to safety. That was all there was to it. "I'm sorry, but I have to make this right."

"I know. If only it weren't so dangerous. If only I weren't so allergic. If only...."

"If I only had a heart," Bethann sang. Oh lord, she thought. I sound just like Mindy. "Listen, I have a Ford truck. Didn't you see those commercials? I'll get through! Nothing can stop me."

"Who's going to go with you?"

"No one. I can't chance taking anyone. What if...?"

Wrong thing to say. "No!"

"Uh...maybe I'll call Mrs. Butchling." She was a trailering veteran, too. Besides, it would be kind of nice to have her along, Bethann decided, giving it more thought. "I'll call you back."

When she hung up and turned around, headed for the ladies room, Mindy, Becky, and Yolanda stood in her way. "You're kidding, right? We're not going with you?"

Bethann held up her hands and started past them. "No. End of discussion."

"You can't do this," Mindy said. "Those are our deer?"

"Oh really, what happened to a minute ago when they were mine, too."

"We're all in this together," Mindy insisted. "We want to go."

"Yeah, well you can't. Look out the window, Mindy. It's a blizzard. *I'm* crazy for going, let alone take all of you, not to mention...." She hesitated, then threw up her hands and stormed into the ladies room, slamming the door behind her.

"Bethann?"

"Oh give me a break. Can I at least pee in peace?"

The girls were lined up on the bench waiting for her when she came out, arms crossed and with defiant looks on their faces.

"Look," Bethann said. "I know how you feel, I do. But the answer is no. If something happens, if I break down, if I get arrested, all of the above, at least I'll know you'll feed the horses and you'll do the medications. I'm really proud of all three of you; I couldn't have gotten through the week without you, but no. The answer is no."

She went into her office and phoned Mrs. Butchling's cell phone, got her voice mail, and left a message. "Everything's okay with Dew Drop, I just need to talk to you. Call me." She hesitated and added, "As s-soon as you can." When she hung up, she started berating herself. Here's this woman, probably at the nursing home after a long hard day at work, a nurse no less, her life in crisis, her husband incurably ill, her whole world falling apart.... And here I am, wanting her to take to the country roads with me and haul a trailer load of deer through a blinding snowstorm. Bethann stared out the window.

Mrs. Butchling phoned right back, and when told, didn't think twice. "I'll be there in an hour."

An hour would be just about perfect. The truck and trailer was stored in the upper barn, that shouldn't be too hard to get out, Bethann told herself. It was downhill from there. Loaded, it would be heavy, there shouldn't be any problems getting back up the hill. It was almost dark out. She could probably load them out front; the girls could herd them right into the back of the trailer. She put on her jacket and gloves and started out the door, but then had a thought.

"Mindy, get Audra on the phone for me," she said, and stopped dead in her tracks. "Oh no, I've become Mom and Dad. Both of them!"

"I thought you didn't need our help."

"Mindy...."

Mindy dialed the phone and handed it to her. "Strange request," Bethann said, when Audra answered. "But is there any way you could plow the back drive by the barn? There's a deer bed back there that has to be demolished. If you can, just push everything over the hill."

"I can try."

"Thanks. How soon...?"

"I don't know, in about an hour, hour and a half."

That would put them leaving here after eight. "Is there any way you can do it any sooner?"

"I'll see what I can do."

"I'll be right back," Bethann told the girls.

"Are we allowed to go in the barn?"

Bethann hesitated, and then nodded, relenting. She felt bad for them, sad. That went without saying. "I know you think I'm being mean...."

"Yes."

"But I'm not. I'm only trying to do what's best, what's safe."

"They're our deer, Bethann," Mindy said. "We love them. We want to go." Yolanda and Becky stood nodding in agreement. "Please."

Bethann shook her head. "You know what? Sooner or later, you're going to have to listen to me. You didn't even practice your violin this week." She looked at Yolanda and

Becky. "And you both know, even if I said yes, your moms aren't going to let you go. Please, I mean it. Give me a break."

Bethann almost welcomed the long walk up the hill. If nothing else, it cleared her head. "I'm forgetting something," she kept saying. She'd gassed the truck up the last time she drove it. She'd even left the trailer hitched. There was no reason to unhitch it at the time, or since. They could double-check it at the barn when she got it down there. Everything seemed in order. "What am I forgetting? Oh no, the CB!"

When she finally got to the upper barn, usually a one-minute walk that was starting to seem like an eternity, she faced frozen doors, another aspect she failed to give thought to until now. "Why me?" she said to herself, pounding on them - and then to the world. "Why me?"

She heard the crunch of footsteps on snow and turned. Mindy, Yolanda, and Becky were coming up the hill after her, and from the sounds of their ensuing laughter, having a grand old time.

"My mom said yes!" Becky said.

"Mine, too!" Yolanda declared.

That left just Mindy. Bethann looked at her. "If you called Mom, I'm going to kill you. I mean it."

Mindy grinned. "Not yet."

Bethann pointed a finger at her, but then gave up for the moment. "You three push and I'll pull," she said, and they all went to work. It was a futile effort. The door didn't even budge.

"All right, move out of the way." Bethann gathered her strength, her wits, her chi, and her lack of sense at the moment, and stepped back and literally threw herself at the door, feet first, with a resounding, "Hi yaa!" When it was all said and done, she was flat on her back in the snow and soon laughing. All three girls started doing the same thing, they were up, they were down, they were up, and they were down. "Hi, yaa! Hi, yaa! Hi, yaa!" And then lo and behold, they heard the ice around the doors snap, and then open.

The truck started right up, Bethann pulled it and the trailer forward. The girls closed the barn doors. Mindy climbed into the front passenger seat, Yolanda and Becky piled in the back seat, and down to the main barn they went. The truck was a Ford 350 crew cab with dual rear tires. The trailer was a six-horse, with side and back loading doors. Bethann weighed the rig once at a semi-truck weigh station; empty it weighed 11,500 pounds. She'd driven it in snow before, though never this much, but felt pretty confident about the way it handled. Unlike the last truck she had, which wasn't very heavy and had no gumption when loaded with horses, this one was, as the commercial said, "Ford Tough." All these considerations went through her mind on the way down the hill, in her efforts to bolster her confidence. She pulled it past the barn, turned it around, and parked it in front of the arena.

"We're going to have to decide how best to pair them up."

"No problem," Mindy said. The three girls had that already figured out. They knew the trailer inside and out, having participated in many shows over the years. And they knew the routine. They checked all the running lights and the brake lights and blinkers while Bethann checked the hitch. They opened the trailer doors and moved the partitions the way they wanted them. It could be a four to six horse in standing stalls, or a two-horse of box stalls. The partitions were heavy-duty gates; that went from floor to ceiling. Bethann had had them custom-made. The girls thought the doe with the newborn fawns should have her own box stall. The rest of the herd could share the other one.

The preparations got to be almost fun after a while. Mindy threw down several bales of hay from the hayloft; the girls dragged them to the trailer and used them for bedding and for the deer to munch on. They opened the underneath compartment and packed it with the rest of the deer pellets and a supply of oats. They filled two five-gallon travel buckets with water, just in case, screwed the lids on tight and tugged and heave-hoed them out to the trailer and loaded them too, and then went inside to warm up.

They were all set, all except for a CB radio.

"I'll bet Howard has one?" Mindy said.

"Call him. If he does, tell him I'll come pick it up."

Mindy got him on the phone. Of course he had one.

"Nerd," Becky and Yolanda said.

Mindy covered the phone and told them to shut up. "He says he can drop it off."

Bethann shook her head. The fewer people knew about this, the better.

"What?" Mindy said. "He's family."

"No he's not." They all laughed, rather giddy at this stage.

"Tell him I'll pick it up in a few minutes. I need to run home anyway." Bethann pointed to Becky and Yolanda, going through a mental checklist. "And I need to talk to both your mothers. Are they at home or at work?"

"Work."

"Get them on the phone." She motioned for Mindy to hurry it up. "Come on, now…before I leave."

Becky and Yolanda's mothers were both excited for the girls, such an adventure: drive careful, I will, call if you need us, do you have money, yes, take your time, our thoughts and prayers are with you, have fun!

"Oh, we'll try," Bethann said. "With any luck, we should be back around one."

"We're spending the night at Mindy's with you," Yolanda said. Becky nodded. They had it all planned. Bethann handed the phone to one of them and started out the door.

"When Mrs. Butchling comes, tell her I'll be right back."

The three girls looked at one another. Mrs. Butchling? They sighed. They'd almost forgotten.

~ 42 ~

Benjamin didn't have the strength to follow Bethann around the house, and sat down in the kitchen. She was gathering bottled water, blankets, crackers, cereal. There weren't many snacks in her parents' house, since Mindy had taken them all with her to Burton when their mother and father left for Europe. Bethann didn't want to have to stop along the way to Susan Nelson's, unless it was for an emergency. If deer were anything like horses, as long as the trailer was moving, they'd have to concentrate on keeping their balance. It was when you stopped for any length of time that things could get a little crazy.

She recalled the day they brought Malaki home. That mare pawed and squealed and whinnied the whole trip. People at the barn said they heard them coming a mile away.

"When's the last time you did the Vicks?"

Benjamin looked at his watch. "Two hours and twenty-two minutes ago."

Bethann smiled. He was so methodical.

"Are you feeling any better, overall?"

He nodded. "But now that I have to worry...."

"No, you don't," Bethann said, kissing him good-bye. "You are in my father's house; I am my father's daughter. All is going to be well."

Benjamin laughed. "Nice try."

"My dad has a bunch of movies."

Benjamin's eyes lit up. "Where?"

"In the den." Bethann ran through a checklist. "Okay, I've got my cell. I have the charger, blankets, snacks." She kissed him again and left. Benjamin watched her car until it drove out of sight, then coughed and sighed and lumbered into the den.

Bethann stopped at Howard's house, picked up the CB and antenna. He gave her a crash course on how to operate it. Everything was falling into place. Mrs. Butchling had just arrived at the barn and, even better, Audra had just finished plowing the back drive. Bethann rolled her window down when Audra slowed to a stop at the top of the hill. She had Sydney with her. "You're good to go," Audra said. "You could drive a semi back there."

Bethann thanked her and waved.

"Bye, Mrs. Sim," Sydney said. "I love the deer."

Bethann drove down the hill, shaking her head; two more accomplices in crime. The girls were anxiously awaiting her return. Mrs. Butchling was squeezing in a little time with Dew Drop. "We're all ready," Mindy said. "The truck's loaded; we've all gone to the bathroom. We've even mixed tomorrow morning's grain and meds, just in case. Let's do it!"

In a perfect world, Bethann would have backed the truck and trailer down behind the barn without any problems. The deer would be enticed to load in the trailer, which after all, didn't look all that much different than the stalls in a barn. They'd bribe them with food. Pixie Dust and the other two youngsters would lead the way. The rest would follow. Then Belle and her two newborn fawns would load. The fawns would be so attached to their dam they would follow her anywhere. The herd would all get comfortable in their surroundings; they'd lie down, eat, nurse, or chew their cud, just as happy as can be, going along for the ride. In a perfect world....

Bethann backed the truck and trailer flush with the back door without too much trouble. It took a little maneuvering, but she had good traction. That was a plus. From the barn to the trailer, was only about a six-inch rise because of the packed snow on the ground; a low step that shouldn't have been any problem for the deer. Nothing should have been a problem. And yet it turned into one problem after another. The deer didn't want any part of the trailer. They didn't even want to look at it. The girls tried enticing Pixie Dust and the other two yearlings with oats, then sweet feed, they rustled the hay, they coaxed, they tried coercing them with sweet talk and promises, and still, the closest they could get them was about ten yards away.

"Turn off the running lights," Mrs. Butchling suggested.

They tried that. Pixie Dust advanced a little more, but still no go. The does in the stall were starting to get a little concerned, restless, and the new momma as well.

"They're afraid," Bethann said. "I don't know of what, but they must be seeing something we're not."

Mrs. Butchling crossed her arms, thinking. "I read a book once about this autistic woman who invented a more humane cow ramp for slaughter."

The girls looked at her as if she were crazy.

"Basically how she discovered it was when she got down to their eye level and could see what was frightening them."

Okay, that made sense. All five of them stooped down and looked into the trailer from the yearling's vantage point, and had to admit, it didn't look like a stall at all. It looked like a trap. Bethann wiped her brow. She was actually sweating. She glanced at her watch. Seven-fifteen.

"Maybe if we put a horse on the one side," Mindy suggested. "And then when this half loads, we can...."

Bethann held up her hand, frowning. "No, let's just try and herd them in. Come on." She motioned for Mindy to get inside the trailer. "Try and guide them to the front, I'd like more weight on the 5th wheel."

Mindy planted herself inside, and Bethann, Yolanda, Becky, and Mrs. Butchling began herding the yearlings toward her. They clapped, they sang, they made swishing noises, they tapped them on the rump. The deer took a few steps toward the trailer, then a few more, and were pretty close when Pixie Dust decided to turn and playfully jog to the other end of the barn, with the other two following.

"Wonderful."

They walked down to shoo them back, and the three youngsters ran back down the aisle way and into the stall with the does. The does weren't budging. "I really think we should try a horse," Mindy insisted. "They don't have any problem going anywhere inside the barn. I think it's because of the horses. I'll get Malaki." Malaki used to be horrible to load, but was an old pro now after having been shown the last couple of years. "What can it hurt to try?"

"Fine." Bethann was ready to wash her hands of the whole mess.

Mindy put a halter and shank on Malaki and led her to the trailer. She never even hesitated. She walked right in, and Mindy closed the gate behind her. "Okay, try now."

Pixie Dust and other two youngsters were already out of the stall and curious. When they started walking toward the trailer, Mrs. Butchling went into the stall with the does, and started urging them out. "Come on," she said. "Let's go. The bus is leaving."

One doe ventured out, Pixie Dust's dam, then another, and like clockwork, the two of them walked right out the backdoor into the trailer. The third one followed, and then here came Pixie Dust and her friends. Mindy nudged them into the stall, closed the gate, and that was that. Surely with Malaki unloaded, the new mom would want to join her herd. As soon as Mindy led Malaki off the trailer, the deer inside started acting up and were soon bouncing off the trailer walls. The yearlings were scared to death, and the adults were stepping all over them.

Mindy turned Malaki around quickly and led her back on, with Malaki snorting, and the deer calmed down instantly.

"Well, I'll be damned," Mrs. Butchling said.

Bethann shook her head. "Now what?" It wouldn't make any sense to take half the herd, and leave the one doe and her two newborn fawns to whatever fate awaited them. That would be like playing God, she thought. No thanks, I don't want the job. "Go get some more hay," she said to the girls.

Becky and Yolanda scrambled to go get a bale.

"What are you going to do?" Mrs. Butchling asked.

"Well…." She looked at Mindy. She looked at the deer. She looked at Malaki. "I'm thinking we should just take her with us. We can put Belle and the two fawns in the middle."

Mindy's eyes widened. "Are you serious?"

Bethann shrugged. "Do you have a better idea?"

Yolanda and Becky spread hay in the middle of the trailer, an area not much smaller than the deer bed. And their attention turned to getting Belle and her newborn fawns to load.

Pixie Dust looked up at Malaki and sneezed, her little nose so cute on the other side of the partition. "Awe…" Mindy said, touching her through the grid before getting off the trailer and out of the way.

When they opened Belle's stall door she walked right out and over to the trailer. She looked first in one direction; Malaki's, and then the other, her herd's, and without a second's hesitation, walked in. In fact she walked in so fast; she banged into the wall and turned around looking rather surprised. The one fawn followed and stood at her side, gazing all around. Two down – one to go. The last one wasn't budging. It appeared weaker than its twin, smaller, and a little wobbly.

"We can't touch her," Bethann cautioned. "Susan said don't touch."

"Him," Mindy said, glancing under his belly. "If we touch him, the dam might reject him. They're still imprinting."

Becky and Yolanda nodded; the three of them had read that. "Come on, little one." They all started clapping their hands softly and clucking. "Come on."

It took one step, changed its mind, and buckled its little knees and laid down, right there in the aisle way. It looked so precious, so cute lying there, but unfortunately now wasn't the time to take a nap. And on such a cold floor yet. Bethann glanced into the blanket room. There probably wasn't a blanket hanging there without some sort of synthetic fiber. "What we need is a wool blanket, and one without any human scent."

The first thought that popped into Mindy's mind and out her mouth was, "How about Leah Oliver's old blanket?"

Bethann looked at her.

"I'm sorry," Mindy said. "But it's 100% wool, it says so right on the tag."

It had been in Bethann's tack trunk forever. "Go get it."

Mindy hurried out of the barn, going as fast as she could, but mindful to not spook the horses, and was back in a flash. "Here."

Bethann drew a deep breath. "All right. We're already messing with Mother Nature, so listen. All of you. If the doe rejects her, him, there's nothing we can do. We're not going to freak out, okay?"

They all nodded apprehensively.

Bethann opened the blanket and covered the fawn completely. And then she and Mrs. Butchling carefully tucked it underneath, and the two of them lifted the little deer. "Be ready to shut the doors," Bethann said. "Get up close."

The girls surrounded them.

Bethann and Mrs. Butchling took measured careful steps to the trailer, not wanting to frighten the dam, or the fawn, and stretched as far as they could inside and laid the second fawn down. "We'll leave the blanket on him," Bethann said, backing up. As the girls closed the doors to the trailer, Belle nosed underneath the blanket and started licking the fawn's face.

Becky and Yolanda turned out all the barn lights, the girls closed the barn doors, and they all piled into the truck. "Do we have everything?" Bethann asked, revving the engine.

The girls nodded.

Mrs. Butchling nodded.

They were all set.

"Okay." As Bethann stared out the windshield into the falling snow, the magnitude of what they were about to undertake washed over her. She hesitated, but only for a second. Now wasn't the time for second-guessing, for doubts, for changing minds. Malaki shifted her weight in the back of the trailer and she felt the tug. Bethann put the truck in low gear, the tires dug in, and they climbed the hill...away from the safety of Maple Dale.

~ 43 ~

Mrs. Butchling made a great co-pilot. She surveyed the maps, went over the routes, and weighed the options. They could take Route 87 to 44 and pick up the turnpike. But turnpikes were scary things to both of them in weather like this. If there was a pileup, they could be stuck for hours, and meanwhile have a circus in the trailer. Not to mention all the highway patrol that was probably out. Bethann was putting a lot of faith in Susan Nelson's sanctioning of this activity, yet still....

"Why don't we take Route 11? Once we're on it, you don't have to get off till our exit."

That choice meant driving a little further out into the wilderness to pick it up, but it made sense. They'd traveled to quite a few horse shows in Youngstown taking Route 11. It was a straight ride, with very little traffic. Bethann agreed. As they crept along Route 87 going about 35 mph, snowdrifts became the biggest challenge. Every time they approached one, Bethann fought the urge to say, "Hold on."

The girls sat in back, oblivious to any danger. They were fascinated with the CB. "Breaker, breaker," Becky said, pretending to call someone. Mindy made a ccchhhh noise. "Come in fourteen."

Mrs. Butchling glanced over her shoulder. "You're supposed to say breaker, breaker one four."

"Oh! Okay. Breaker, breaker, come in one four."

More ccchhhh noise from Mindy.

"No, say breaker, breaker, one four, come in."

"Okay. Breaker, breaker, one four, come in, one four."

Yolanda yawned.

It took an hour and half to get from Maple Dale to Route 11, a drive under normal conditions that would have taken on average about thirty-five minutes. Fortunately they were able to pick up the pace a little on the highway. Bethann tucked their truck and trailer in between two semis and felt rather snug. If the semi in front of her passed a vehicle, she also passed the vehicle, and the semi behind her did the same.

"I wonder if we can get them on the CB," Mindy said.

"No," Bethann said. "Don't even try."

"Come on, don't you think it'd be fun to let them know we're all girls."

"Oh yeah, that sounds like something we'd want to announce."

They all laughed, then rode for a while listening to the radio, and to Yolanda's snoring. Becky nudged her.

"What?"

"Cut it out. You sound like my dad."

Mindy glanced behind them at the trailer. "Does everything seem all right back there?"

Bethann nodded. If a horse or horses, or in this case, a horse and a herd of deer, are restless, you could feel it in the way the truck handles. "They're probably all sleeping."

"And snoring," Becky said.

Yolanda pushed her. "Leave me alone."

Bethann and Mrs. Butchling chuckled.

Time to pass another car. Bethann followed the truck and was tucked back in. "I'm going to hate to see these guys leave." They were coming up on Youngstown and chances were that's where these trucks would be getting off. Sure enough, they slowed to an almost crawl to make the loop. When both trucks turned on their blinkers to take their exit, Bethann flashed her lights to say thank you. The girls waved to them when they flashed their lights back.

The road ahead was pitch black, not a car in sight. "Do you want me to take over?" Mrs. Butchling asked.

"No, I'm okay." Bethann said, with a nervous smile. Right about then the radio reception faded. Mrs. Butchling tried to find another station. It was all-static.

"Maybe we can sing," Mindy said, and went right into "Take me home, country roads...." The girls joined in. "To the place, I belong...." Mrs. Butchling laughed. "West Virginia, mountain momma, take me home, country roads."

"You're not going to believe this," Bethann said, her knuckles white on the steering wheel. "But I sang that same song earlier today, and here we are, taking that country road to West Virginia. Wow, what are the odds of that?"

Amazing, Mindy thought, and leaned forward to ask Mrs. Butchling a question. "Did you know Leah Oliver?"

"Just in passing," she said. "I met her on an excursion to the Coliseum to see the Lipizzaners."

"You're kidding?" Bethann said. "I was there, too. I was just a kid."

"Oh go ahead, rub it in."

Bethann smiled. "This is so unbelievable." She'd only known Mrs. Butchling the last six years or so. "Just this morning when I was talking to Winnie I thought about that day! Wow!" She got chills.

"What are you saying?" Mrs. Butchling asked. "That we were all destined to be on this God-forsaken desolate road together tonight?"

They all laughed. Then the girls decided they were hungry and started going through the snacks. "Do you want anything?"

"No," Mrs. Butchling said. Bethann declined also. There was no way she was going to take her hands off the steering wheel. While the girls ate and chatted amongst themselves, Bethann took the opportunity to talk in relative privacy with Mrs. Butchling.

"I told my dad about your situation."

Mrs. Butchling nodded slightly, staring out the side window.

"He says he thinks someone's pulling some scare tactics on you, and says not to do anything till he comes back. He wants to see all your insurance policies."

"Thank you, and thank him too, but I can't afford to...."

"There's no charge."

Mrs. Butchling sighed. "I hate charity."

"It's not charity. You want to know what charity is, you right here. I never doubted for a second that you'd come."

Mrs. Butchling just looked at her for a moment and then patted her gently on the arm, unable to speak.

Mindy glanced from one to the other. She'd heard and observed the exchange between them, and was so moved, she reached behind the back seat and took out her violin case. She could be so dramatic. Bethann smiled when she heard her warming up. She hadn't realized she'd brought the violin with her. Mrs. Butchling glanced over her shoulder. "What the...?"

"Bethann told me I had to practice," Mindy said, grinning. Mindy sat forward and then back, to get comfortable. She rocked from side to side, loosening up while deciding what to play. It would have to be something she knew by heart, maybe something from the Christmas recital. It seemed a fitting choice, with all the snow. She set her jaw and raised the bow while drawing a deep cleansing breath. Find your space; find your center, she told herself. Breathe. Breathe. And when ready, she began to play one of the most beautiful songs on earth.

"Silent night. Holy night. All is calm, all is bright. Round yon virgin, mother and child. Holy infant so tender and mild. Sleep in heavenly peace.... Sleep in heavenly peace."

Bethann and Mrs. Butchling sang the words softly, Yolanda and Becky, too.

"Silent night. Holy night. Shepherds quake at the sight. Glories stream from heaven afar. Heavenly hosts sing alleluia. Christ, the Savior is born.... Christ, the Savior is born."

There were distant cars up ahead.

"Silent night, holy night. Son of God, love's pure light. Radiant beams from Thy holy face. With the dawn of redeeming grace. Jesus Lord at Thy birth.... Jesus Lord at Thy birth."

Everyone hummed the last verse again. No one wanted the moment to end. Jesus Lord, at Thy birth.... Jesus Lord, at Thy birth.

They rode for a while in complete silence, the lights up ahead growing brighter and brighter through the falling snow. Cars, trucks, people, a rest stop.

"Does anyone have to go?" Bethann asked, with obvious hesitation in her voice.

The girls all looked at one another and then at Mrs. Butchling; sitting there quietly. "We do," they said, all three of them at the same time for her sake. Bethann put on her blinker, pulled to a stop at the concession area to drop them off, and drove on to the service area to top off the gas tank. Things were quiet in the trailer. Things were quiet everywhere, just the sound of tires crunching on snow.

"Ma'am," she heard someone say.

She turned. A tiny little woman was peering over the side of her open car window. An elderly man sat at the wheel. "We've been following you since Route 76. Thank you. You're a darned good little driver. We just wanted to let you know."

"Thank you." Malaki nickered at the sound of Bethann's voice. "It's okay, girl," she said, smiling as she pressed her hand gently to the side of the trailer. "Everything's okay." She'd been so intent on there being no one on the road ahead of her; she'd never even looked to see if there had been anyone behind them.

"There's usually a lot of traffic from this point on. Thank you." Bethann smiled and waved to the old couple, paid for her gas, and pulled the rig back around to the concession area.

Mrs. Butchling was waiting for her. "They're buying candy," she said, shaking her head. "Do you want me to drive for a while?"

"No, I'm fine. Thanks. How much further you think?"

Mrs. Butchling looked at the map. "I'd say maybe about an hour."

"Maybe I'd better go to the ladies room. That standing out in the cold did me in."

The trailer rocked a little.

"I'll circle the parking lot," Mrs. Butchling said, and slid over behind the wheel.

Bethann met up with the girls on their way out. "She'll be back around in a second. Stay inside," she said. The girls were all eating ice cream sandwiches. A few minutes later, Bethann was back behind the wheel and they were on the road again.

~ 44 ~

One would think the further south they drove, the less snow they would encounter. But that was not the case. Even the girls started paying attention to the road conditions. As predicted by the elderly couple at the rest stop, there was an increase in traffic. Bethann couldn't decide what was worse under the circumstances, no one on the road in front of her, or an abundance of drivers riding their brakes. It was a toss-up.

"You girls are in your seatbelts, right?"

"Yes," they said, and all double-checked.

Bethann and Mrs. Butchling both instinctively tugged on their own as well.

"My brother says seatbelts do more harm than good," Yolanda said.

"Well, that's simply not true," Mrs. Butchling stated. "How old is your brother?"

"Seventeen."

Mrs. Butchling nodded. "Hmph." Enough said.

"He says that lots of times people get trapped or crushed in their cars, where, if they were thrown free...."

Mrs. Butchling shuddered.

"He says that his friend George would not be alive today if he was wearing a seatbelt. When his car was hit, he was thrown out the windshield and the driver side of the car was all caved in. He would have been pulverized."

"For every one of those cases, there are hundreds to the contrary," Mrs. Butchling insisted.

"Yeah, but...." Yolanda said, with Becky and Mindy nodding in support.

Mrs. Butchling glanced at them. "Is the reason he doesn't want to wear one, because he actually thinks he's going to get in an accident and get crushed?"

"Uh...." Yolanda looked at Mindy and Becky. "I guess. Otherwise, why would he...?"

"I would assume, since most teens think they are going to live forever, that it's more about being cool, about image. I wish I had a dollar for every mangled teen I've seen come through emergency."

Yolanda fell silent. She'd forgotten about the woman being a nurse, Mindy and Becky, too.

Mrs. Butchling stared out her side window. "My son died in a car accident."

The girls remained silent. They didn't have to ask to know; he wasn't wearing his seatbelt.

"But that's okay. He was cool."

"I'm sorry," Bethann said. "I didn't know you had a son."

"Randy," Mrs. Butchling said. "He was sixteen."

"Was he an only child?"

Mrs. Butchling hesitated. "At the time," she said. She pressed her hand to the side of her face, wondering how she'd gotten into this conversation. She usually kept things to herself. "I had a daughter. She drowned at summer camp as a child. She was my oldest. We just had the two."

Yolanda swallowed hard and shook her head. "I'm sorry."

"Me, too," Mindy said.

"Me, too," Becky echoed softly.

"So, here I am a nurse and...." Mrs. Butchling shrugged, a helpless gesture, a helpless feeling. She'd tragically lost both of her children in an instant, and now she was dealing with the loss of her husband, little by little, day by day. "I don't know what's worse," she said.

They rode in silence for miles - and then up ahead, a sign slowly came into view. "PIEDMONT NEXT EXIT" They'd been on the road close to three hours, with thirty miles left to go. "When you get off, you're going to take a left," Mrs. Butchling said.

Bethann nodded.

"You know, I just had a thought," Mindy said. "We're kind of like a deer herd in a deer bed, here in this truck. We're does and yearlings up front, and does and yearlings in the back." They all laughed. "I'm serious. We all fit. We can't stand and we can't move around, but we all fit. I think that's pretty cool." They all agreed.

Bethann put her blinker on, exited Route 11, and turned left. "Oh boy!" she said, surveying what lay ahead. Some two-lane highways have wide shoulders and some have none. The one they were on now had none. And judging from the looks of it, it probably hadn't been plowed for hours.

"Is it too late to change our minds?" Mrs. Butchling asked.

Everyone chuckled nervously, having similar thoughts. "We'll just have to go a little slower," Bethann said. When she stopped at the light, she slid halfway through the intersection. She'd never driven any distance in low range four-wheel drive, but low range four-wheel drive it was going to have to be. She felt a little tug from the trailer. "We're almost there, girl," she said, as if Malaki could hear her.

Mrs. Butchling tried the radio again and found a country western station with fairly decent reception. "'Cause I've got friends in low places...." The girls started singing along with Garth Brooks. The station quickly switched to static, and then nothing.

"Awe, bummer."

Mrs. Butchling tried another. "It would be nice to get the weather."

"Snow and cold," Mindy said, raising her arms and imitating Bill Murray from the movie "Groundhog Day." "The winds will be coming in from the north, and swoop down...."

Yolanda and Becky pushed at her, laughing. They'd seen that movie almost as many times as "Sleepless in Seattle."

Mrs. Butchling scanned through the channels twice, and still couldn't find a station coming in clear. There were a few where they could make out a word or two, a piece of melody, but nothing consistent. Bethann suggested she just turn it off. It was making her nervous.

Twenty-two miles to go. The houses were far apart, about a quarter of a mile from one to the next. There were lights on in just about every one of them. The girls counted fourteen houses in a row with satellite dishes, all pointing north.

Bethann felt another tug from the trailer, glanced in both side mirrors and kept driving. Whatever it was would have to wait. She wasn't stopping. "See if you can get the CB to work."

The girls fought over it.

"Cut it out," Bethann said.

Yolanda ended up with it.

"Breaker, breaker one four, come in one four."

Nothing. Not even static.

"Are you sure you have it on?"

"Put the window down a little." When Yolanda rolled the window down, a blast of cold air hit them in the face.

"Breaker, breaker, one four, come in one four."

"Ccchhhh!"

Everyone jumped in their seats. The CB was on full volume. It was so loud; Malaki and the deer probably heard it. Yolanda turned it down, laughing. "Breaker, breaker, one four, come in one four."

"Breaker, breaker, one four, out."

The girls clapped.

"Um, do we keep saying breaker, breaker?"

Mrs. Butchling shook her head.

"What do we want?" Yolanda asked.

"Sassie Susie," Bethann said. "Ask for Sassie Susie."

"I'm looking for Sassie Susie, out."

"Sassie Susie?" It was a man's voice. "What do you want with that old broad? Out."

"Uh...."

"Uh...."

"Tell them we're on our way to see her, and need to know uh...the road conditions." Bethann shrugged. "Come on you guys, think of something. I shouldn't have to do this, I'm driving."

There was no need to come up with anything. All they had to do was listen.

"Don't you call me an old broad, you old fool. Out."

Bethann laughed. "That's Sassy Susie!"

"Where are you? Out."

"Tell her we're on Route 33, about four maybe five miles this side, east of 98," Mrs. Butchling said, looking at the map.

"We're about five miles east of 98."

"On Route 33," Mrs. Butchling insisted she say.

"On Route 33. Out."

"Good, you haven't gotten to the bridge yet."

Oh God, Bethann said, this was like a bad dream. If she says the bridge is out, I'm going to scream.

"When you get to the bridge, look for a red pickup. Out."

"Okay." Yolanda shrugged. "Uh…. Out."

Becky and Mindy laughed. "So much for being a CB know-it-all now."

"Shhhh," Bethann said.

"That'll be Big Dave. Out."

Yolanda hesitated, getting a little flustered. "Uh…out," she repeated.

Becky and Mindy laughed again.

"Shut up," Bethann said. "I mean it."

"The bridge is out, so he's gonna take you a different way. Out."

Bethann put her head down in disbelief, but then quickly catching herself, glued her eyes back to the road.

"Don't panic, now. Out."

Silence….

Panic….

"It's a rough road and it's gonna take you a little longer. Out."

Bethann stared straight ahead. Was it a coincidence or was it starting to snow harder? She asked Mrs. Butchling. Mrs. Butchling nodded. It *was* snowing harder.

"This is a joke. What did we do to deserve this?"

"What do we do to deserve anything?"

Bethann glanced at her. Good point.

"There have been many times in my life, I've felt like Job. Job has nothing on me." Mrs. Butchling laughed, perhaps laughing in the face of adversity. "Yep, here we are…Job, Jobie, and the Jobettes!" They all laughed at that.

"Oh no, look," Bethann said, pointing. Their mouths dropped. Up ahead in the road, stood a big buck. It was in the other lane, but slowly ambling toward theirs.

If you see a deer, don't swerve, Bethann recited in her head. Anyone living in the country knows that sad reality. Swerve and you're liable to end up in a ditch. Not an entertaining scenario for anyone let alone a driver hauling a heavy load. Bethann slowed as best she could, she couldn't hit the brakes too hard, not with the ice and snow. "Pray," she said. "Pray, pray, pray."

The girls started right up. "The Lord is my shepherd I shall not want."

Bethann applied a little more pressure on the brakes.

"Gently," Mrs. Butchling cautioned, darting her eyes from the deer to Bethann's foot.

"He maketh me to lie down in green pastures. He leadeth me beside still waters."

"Gently...."

"He restoreth my soul. He leadeth me in the path of righteousness for His name's sake."

The deer stood watching their approach.

"Yea, though I walk through the valley of the shadow of death, I fear no evil."

Bethann pressed the brake a little more and felt a tug from behind. There'd be no way she could stop.

"For thou are with me. Thy rod and Thy staff shall comfort me."

Bethann glanced at the dashboard. They were going 18 mph. If they hit him at that speed, could he survive? Would the truck stay on a straight course? Would he hit the windshield?

"Surely goodness and mercy shall follow me all the days of my life, and I shall dwell in the house of the Lord forever."

The girls held their breath. They were only about twenty yards from the buck.

"Honk at him," Mindy said.

Bethann shook her head. If she laid on her horn, what would Malaki and the deer in the trailer do? She couldn't chance sounding a warning that could cause harm to an even greater number of animals. If the herd panicked, they could flip the trailer.

The buck stood in the road, smack dab in the middle of their lane. He stood tall and proud, and stared. He stared into Bethann's eyes. He stared into Mrs. Butchling's eyes. He stared into Mindy and Yolanda's and Becky's eyes. They were going to hit him.

"Oh my God!" the girls cried.

Bethann braced herself. Mrs. Butchling braced herself.

At the last possible second, the buck turned and ran out of the way.

The truck and trailer wheels rolled over the exact spot where he'd been standing.

The girls squealed with excitement, all talking at the same time. "Oh my God! Oh my God! Oh my God! Did you see that?"

"He looked at me!"

"He looked at me!"

"He looked at me, too!"

"Give me a bottle of water," Bethann said. Her throat was so dry she could hardly swallow. Mrs. Butchling handed her one and motioned for the girls to calm down. The silence that followed gave each pause for individual reflection.

Bethann drank half the bottle of water without stopping, without breathing, and then quickly handed the bottle back to Mrs. Butchling. There was trouble up ahead; two police cars sat in the road, lights flashing. Bethann slowed to a stop and rolled down her window. "I'll do the talking," she said, as one of the officers approached the truck.

"Ma'am."

"What seems to be the problem?"

"You mean in addition to the weather and people not supposing to be out on the road?" He shielded his face from the blinding snow. "Where are you all from?"

"Uh, Ohio, R-Russell," she said, correcting herself. This still was Ohio.

The officer nodded knowingly. "That's up there in Geauga County, correct?"

Bethann's heart dropped. She feared the next thing out of his mouth and imagined it being, "We're going to have to confiscate your trailer and take those deer off your hands. Follow us, please."

But he didn't say that. He didn't say that at all.

"You're going to have to turn around and head on back. There's a road ban about to go into effect."

"Okay," Bethann said, reluctantly, trying to judge the turn-around space. When the officer tapped the door, apparently his way of saying good-bye, Mindy leaned forward. They didn't come this far for nothing.

"Big Dave is waiting for us at the bridge," she said, like it was some sort of code.

"Oh, he is, now is he?" The officer looked in at her.

If this man wasn't a Susan Nelson fan, they were in big trouble, because Mindy proceeded to tell him that's where they were headed.

"You don't say?"

"She's only, how far?" She looked at Mrs. Butchling.

"Twelve miles," she replied.

"See, not far at all."

Malaki whinnied right about then. Leave it to her to whinny when she heard voices, let alone Mindy's, one she knew. Typical of her, she promptly started pawing when she didn't get a reply, and the trailer started rocking.

"She's not a good shipper," Mindy said. "Please."

The man stepped back and motioned for them to go. He didn't say which way, so Bethann took a chance. She drove around the barricade and kept right on going. "Are they coming after us?" she asked, afraid to look in the side mirrors herself.

"No," Mrs. Butchling said. "He's just standing in the road."

"I can't take any more of this," Bethann said, clutching the steering wheel. "I honestly can't."

Mrs. Butchling smiled at her. "What, are you kidding me? This is most fun I've had in years."

The girls laughed. Even Bethann laughed a little.

"Is he still standing there?" she asked. She glanced in the mirror herself, but couldn't see. Neither could Mrs. Butchling at this point. They took that as a good sign. If he'd decided to come after them, surely they would have been able to at least see his headlights. The bridge and Big Dave was less than a mile and a half away....

~ 45 ~

If Big Dave's truck was a boat, and it certainly had the size, it could be said that it was lit from stem to stern. "Oh my God." The girls gasped; Bethann and Mrs. Butchling's sentiments exactly. It had an array of hood lights, in addition to running lights above and beneath the cab, and rows of lights down the side of the bed and bed cap. A huge spotlight mounted vertically on the bumper illuminated a widespread set of longhorn cow horns on the grill, giving off a rather mystical impression that perhaps the cow had ascended to greener pastures.

"Turn around," Mindy said, as they drew closer.

There were at least two dozen sets of trophy deer racks mounted on the back of the truck bed.

"I said turn around."

Bethann told her to be quiet. "I mean it, shut up right now." Surely they hadn't come all this way under the worst possible conditions to have their deer harmed, she told herself. Surely Winnie wouldn't have set her off on a path to the deer's destruction.

Big Dave got out of his truck and waved.

"Oh my God."

He was a giant of a man, tall and heavy, and had a big gray beard. Bethann slowed to a stop and lowered her window.

"Howdy, Ma'am," he said.

Bethann nodded. Mrs. Butchling stared. The girls stared.

"It's about twenty miles, the way we're going to go, but it's the only way with the bridge out."

Bethann nodded again. The man looked nice enough, in a rough kind of way.

"You got your CB?"

Bethann nodded again.

"Okay, let's go. You got my handle, it's Big Dave," he said. "You'll be fine. Don't worry." He patted her door, just like the cop, and then hesitated before he walked toward his truck. "Nice rig."

"Thank you."

Having to follow the remains of two dozen deer and a dead cow for the next twenty miles did not bode well. Mindy started "freaking out," as her mother would say. "I want to talk to Sassy Susie! Get her on the CB."

Bethann shook her head. What was it with their family, when in times of crisis, that they couldn't dial their own phone, their own CB...? She laughed to herself, and when everyone looked at her as if she'd lost her mind, apologized. "I'm sorry, but you sounded just like dad."

"Can we call him?" Mindy said.

"Oh no."

"Can we call Sassy Susie?"

Mrs. Butchling looked at her. "Anything you say, Big Dave's going to hear."

Mindy could hardly stand to look at his truck. "Do we have to follow so close?"

"Yes," Bethann said.

"They're lit up like a Christmas tree."

"Deer shed their antlers," Mrs. Butchling said.

"I know that," Mindy said, and no sooner said, reached up and hugged her. "Oh my God, thank you. I'd forgotten!"

Mrs. Butchling seemed taken aback with the hug at first, but then patted her arm. She seemed a lot like Malaki that way. Mindy sat back happy. Yolanda and Becky were equally relieved. They'd all read the same article about male deer shedding their antlers every year after rutting season as a result of lower testosterone levels. The discarded racks can be found anywhere. The three of them were so shocked by the sight of the deer antlers, all they'd seen at first, was death, killing.

"I wonder if cows shed their horns?" Mindy said.

Mrs. Butchling sighed. "No."

"Ccchhhhh...." The CB crackled.

Yolanda turned up the volume. It was Big Dave letting Sassie Susie know he'd "hooked up with the trailer."

"How are the roads?"

"Not good."

"I'll put some coffee on."

"We'll see you in about an hour."

Bethann and Mrs. Butchling and the girls experienced a range of emotions during this exchange. Happiness, comfort, they felt safe, then not so safe, and ultimately, they all sunk deeper and deeper into their seats in disappointment. An hour?

"I have to pee," Yolanda said.

"This sucks."

"My legs hurt."

"My butt hurts."

"Do we have any more pretzels?"

"No, just crackers."

Mrs. Butchling glanced at Bethann and smiled. "You're doing good," she said softly.

Bethann relaxed a little. "Thank you," she replied, for everything. For a little over ten miles, they just followed along, without incident. The girls ate every last crumb of food in the truck, they listened to some CB conversations between two truckers. Bethann eventually told them turn it off. It was getting a little R-rated.

"But we won't be able to hear Sassie Susie or Big Dave if we need to."

"Then turn it down." It started snowing even harder. Another mile and even the lights from Big Dave's truck were hard to see.

"Ccchhhhhhh."

Yolanda turned up the volume on the CB.

"I think we're going to need a little help," they heard Big Dave say, and then Sassie Susie's crusty voice. "I'll see what I can do."

Bethann glanced at her odometer. To have gotten this far and then to not be able to…. Her cell phone rang, startling her, along with everyone else in the truck. She refused to take her hands off the wheel. Mindy answered it. "Hello." She paused. "It's Benjamin." She held the phone to Bethann's ear.

"We're fine, we're almost there. No, no…everything's f-fine."

"Liar, liar, pants on fire," the girls whispered to one another.

"What? Oh brother, what did you tell them?" She glanced at Mindy. "Mom and dad called. Okay, fine. We'll call you when we get there. I love you."

Mindy sat back and closed the phone. "I just won't answer it," she said.

"What, and so they get on the next plane."

The phone rang instantly.

"Hi, Mom!" Mindy said. "Oh, just a feeling."

The girls chuckled.

"No, we're fine. Where are we? Uh…we're on our way to the uh…the barn." She shrugged. It wasn't a lie, actually. "Snowing? Yes, it's still snowing. Bethann? Well, she's driving. Okay, hold on?" Bethann shook her head no. "No!"

Mindy held the phone to her ear. "Hey, Mom, is Dad there? Can I talk to him? Mrs. Butchling's here and I thought maybe Dad could talk to her."

Mrs. Butchling started shaking *her* head no.

"Hi, Dad. Here she is. No, no…everything's f-fine. Talk to her."

Mindy held the phone to Mrs. Butchling's reluctant ear.

"Hello," she said, and then, "Okay." She took the phone from Mindy. Her hands were free; there was no reason to…. "Life insurance, me? Yes. I don't know, a hundred thousand. The standard, I guess. Okay." She listened. "Thank you."

She handed the phone to Mindy. "Hi, Dad. Oh…Hi, Mom! We'll call you tomorrow." She motioned for Mindy and Yolanda to say something.

"Bye, Mrs. Morrison!"

"Bye, Mom!"

Mindy closed the phone shut and sat back pleased with herself. "Well, that went well," she said, and everyone laughed. Not two seconds later, they heard a roaring kind of motor sound coming from behind them and then another to the side of them, and another and another. Snowmobiles!

"Oh God, if they cut in front of me, I'm gonna die," Bethann said. The girls counted them; one, two, three, four...here came some more, five, six, seven, eight.... The snowmobilers zoomed past them, waved, and then past Big Dave. He blinked his lights, a thank you. They weren't trouble. They were there to show the way.

Tears welled up in Bethann's eyes. They were going to make it after all. For the first time since leaving Maple Dale, she had no doubt. They were going to make it and everything was going to be okay.

Mrs. Butchling privately handed her a tissue.

"Thank you," she said.

Fifteen minutes later, after creeping along at about 10 mph, Big Dave put on his turn signal, blinked his lights again, and the snowmobilers drove on. Susan's driveway was winding and long. But like the light at the end of the tunnel, her house sat as a beacon at its end.

Bethann followed Big Dave past the house to the barn, and when he got out and motioned, she pulled the truck and trailer up close. Sassie Susie came out to greet them, wiping her hands and all smiles. "You made it," she said.

"Yep, we made it."

Malaki whinnied.

~ 46 ~

Susan Nelson kept introductions short and sweet. "I'm Susie," she said, and when Malaki whinnied again and started pawing. "I wasn't expecting a horse."

Bethann smiled. "She just came along for the ride," she said, and gave a brief, very brief explanation. "With any luck, we have a doe in the center with her two fawns. The rest of the herd is up front and Malaki's in the back."

"Nice name. You say the deer are used to a barn, right?"

The girls nodded. The barn was huge, one of those big old cow barns.

211

"All right, let's get them out. I've got a stall for them just inside."

"Would you happen to have two?" Mindy asked.

Sassie Susie looked at her. "This ain't the Hilton."

"I know, but…" Mindy said, rather sheepishly, snow falling all around them. "The doe is still imprinting, and…."

"I'm just kidding you, honey. Come on, we'll figure something out. Dave," she said. "Move those two kids out of the run-in."

"Kids?"

"Goats, honey. Goats."

Bethann cracked opened the side door on the trailer and made the girls stand back so she and Mrs. Butchling could peek in first, just in case. "They're fine. They're fine," Mrs. Butchling said, with a thumbs-up. The doe stood watch over her two fawns. Malaki seemed none the worse for wear. And all seven deer in front were on their feet.

"All right, let's form a human barricade," Susie said. "We'll put the doe and her fawns in the stall, and the rest of the herd in the run-in."

Bethann opened the door wide and the girls flanked one side, Mrs. Butchling and Bethann the other. Susie stood close to the trailer and started humming and making a really strange clicking noise with her tongue. The doe looked at her. The fawns looked at her. All seven deer up front looked at her. Malaki looked at her.

"She's Morgan, right? Very pretty."

Mindy nodded proudly.

"Come on, Momma," Susie said, to the doe.

"Come on, Belle," the girls said. "It's all right."

"Ahhh…you name an animal and they're with you for life, even when they die," Susie said. "Come on, Belle."

Belle nuzzled her fawns and raised her head. When Susie started humming again, Belle walked toward her, stepped down off the trailer and the one fawn followed. The other one just stood there, causing Belle some concern. She turned back and lowered her head.

"We had to pick him up to load him," Bethann said.

"I'll get him," Mrs. Butchling said, the closest to the trailer. She carefully picked up the blanket, so as not to scare the fawn or alarm Belle, and covered the fawn and picked him up in her arms. "Lead the way," she said, and followed. Belle was perfectly happy to walk into the barn and into her new stall. To look at her weary expression, she'd probably stood the entire trip, watching dutifully over her newborn young. The stall was nice and big, and bed knee-deep in straw. Mrs. Butchling put the fawn down in the center of it, took the blanket off of him, and Belle lowered her head and started nuzzling her babe. Its twin laid down right next to him, two little bundles of fur. Belle nuzzled her, too.

Susie turned. "Dave? You ready?"

"Yep," he yelled. "Bring 'em on."

The girls were right on her heels as she headed for the trailer. "What's that clicking thing you were doing?"

"Ah, that. Some of 'em listen, some of 'em don't. Not every animal speaks my language," she said.

The girls laughed, walking along with her.

Bethann and Mrs. Butchling followed, taking in all the cobwebs and clutter and disrepair. The barn looked to be a hundred years old if a day, and had love - but hard times written all over it. Mindy climbed up in the trailer, waited until everyone was in place, and then waited for Susie to give the okay. Little Pixie Dust sneezed.

"Well, hello to you, too," Susie said.

The girls looked at one another, beaming. The sneezing *was* a way of talking.

"All right, are we all set? Okay, open the door."

The first one out, coming as no surprise, was Pixie Dust, her little tail swishing. The other two yearlings were right behind her, then Pixie Dust's dam, and finally the rest. They all stepped down out of the trailer, like they were going for a Sunday walk. Pixie Dust jogged down the aisle way as if she'd been there all her life. Sneeze - sneeze, swish - swish, ah choo, ah choo, ah choo.

Big Dave stood at the end, arms out and pointing, and one by one, they filed past him and out into the run-in. When the last one was safe and secure, Susie closed the gate and everyone drew a collective breath and sighed. Right about then, Malaki started whinnying again, and got louder and louder.

"Do you mind if we walk her up and down the aisle way a couple of times?" Bethann asked. "Give her some exercise."

"Nah, that's fine. I've got coffee made. We can put her in a stall on the other side so you all can take a little rest as well."

Mindy went to get Malaki, led her off the trailer, and while she walked her up and down the aisle way, Becky and Yolanda, Mrs. Butchling, and Bethann got the grand tour of this side of the barn. There were the two kids, rescues, a calf, she's blind, a jersey milk cow, sheep, sheep, and more sheep, I spin my own wool, it's how I pay the bills. Some llamas, and a three-legged alpaca, another rescue, why would anyone do that, horrible, then a pony that looked like it had seen better times, he'll be okay, he went a long time without food, it's going to take a while, his stable mate didn't make it, if I had a gun, I'd shoot those people. There were countless chickens, they lay green eggs, no I'm not kidding, and they're really good, a goose, no, she doesn't lay gold eggs, I wish she did, and an egret, you didn't see her, I can't stand the thought of anyone taking care of her but me, I'm real attached to that one, look at the way she looks at me, that's nice, you see it, too. The egret fanned its wings and ducked and bobbed its head.

Mindy and Malaki met up with them, Malaki was getting harder and harder to walk; she was all wound up, snorting and prancing. "Come on, follow me," Susie said. The aisle way to the other side was even more cluttered. It was an obstacle course. Malaki looked wary, snorting even louder. She didn't want any part of it and started backing up – wide eyed. No way.

But then she heard a horse nicker. She raised her head and whinnied, the horse whinnied back. Then it was almost like, get out my way, she was going to the other side. Mindy laughed. There were three horses over there. One was a palomino with a huge scar across its face. Susie shook her head. "I'll spare you the details on that one." The next was "an old gray mare" just like the song, with years and years of sadness in her eyes. "Ah, don't let her fool you; she's happy as can be now. She just wants a peppermint." Susie had a supply of them in her pocket, gave some to the girls and the old gray mare perked right up. "See what I mean."

The last one, the one whinnying and nickering, was a huge thoroughbred. He stood about 17.1, was all black with a tiny white star on its forehead, and looked young, the picture of health. "Now that one; that one's my fault. I don't know what to do with him. He's just too much horse for me. I bought him off the track last year down at Mountaineer. I didn't like the son of a bitch who was training him. He was going to break him down, running him the way he was, and...."

Malaki snorted at him, gave him that wide-eyed look of hers, and Mindy quickly led her away before she started squealing. Malaki went reluctantly, looking back at him and whinnying and whinnying. The stall next to him was empty, the two horses couldn't see each other, but could certainly smell one another. They both sniffed and snorted, and the thoroughbred took to bucking and kicking in his stall.

"What's his name?" Bethann asked.

"Well, I call him Shit-ass. Pardon me," she said to the girls. They all laughed. "But his registered name is Easy To Do." She paused, shaking her head. "Boy, is that a joke."

Bethann looked in at him. "What have you done with him since you bought him?"

"Well, you mean aside from trying to keep all four of his feet on the ground and me on his back?"

Bethann chuckled. The girls and Mrs. Butchling, too.

"Frankly, I've just been trying to find him a home."

Bethann stared in at him; bucking and playing. If what she was feeling wasn't love at first sight, it was pretty darn close. "Do you mind if I...?" She wanted to go in and look him over.

"Uh...." Susie shrugged, shaking her head. "Be my guest."

Bethann reached for his halter and shank and opened the stall door, oblivious to anyone else in the barn, any other horse, any other animal. It was just her and Easy To Do. He settled down enough for her to put on his halter, but then started acting up. Malaki wasn't helping with her antics on the other side of the wall. Bethann shanked him a couple of times to get his attention. He stood tall - looking at her, and watched her every move as she ran her hand down his legs. Knees and ankles, fine. She checked his stifles for soreness. As tall as he was, they were probably a problem, racing. She checked his hocks. Then she checked his teeth. She checked his back. He didn't flinch, he didn't move. The year off had apparently done him wonders. He looked sound as could be.

When she let go of his lead shank and stepped back to gaze at him from a distance, he lowered his head and walked over to her. And it was the way he lowered his head that won her over entirely. When she reached up and stroked his face, he pressed against her hand...a gentle action that brought tears to Bethann's eyes.

~ **47** ~

Sassie Susie's farmhouse looked exactly like one would imagine, cluttered, mismatched, and as warm and welcoming as can be. She had a big potbelly stove fired up in the living room and another one in the kitchen. "Cream and sugar?"

"Yes, please."

"What about you three?" She glanced at Mindy, Yolanda, and Becky. "Hot cocoa?" They nodded, took off their boots and coats, and formed a line behind Mrs. Butchling for the bathroom. "It's right down the hall."

When they all appeared in the kitchen, with Mindy, Yolanda, and Becky each holding one of the many resident cats, Susie looked at them and shook her head. "I see myself in every one of you. God help ya."

They laughed, and she motioned for them all to sit down. Big Dave was already helping himself to a piece of Boston cream pie. He looked like a jolly old Santa on Christmas morning. He even wore suspenders. Susie looked tiny standing next to him, was probably only five foot tall if that, and had snow-white hair bound in a clip. Her baggy jeans suggested she might have been heavy once upon a time; she had on two flannel shirts and a turtleneck sweater, and visible arthritis in her hands. She placed mugs and saucers in front of them. "How about some cheese and crackers? Dave."

He pulled some cheese out of the fridge and Susie searched through her silverware drawer for a cheese knife, and set out a box of crackers. The girls helped themselves. When they had all gotten their coffee and cocoa, Susie sat down and started slicing each of them a hardy piece of the Boston cream pie. "Before Dave eats it all."

They all laughed again, Big Dave included. Conversation came easy. It was as if they'd all known one another all their lives. Susie wasn't a propagator, like Winnie. She was officially a "wildlife rehabilitator."

"I started out with this one fawn, the cutest little thing. It wasn't but a day or two old, when some asshole hunter...sorry," she said. "Anyway, the doe was gone and I took in the fawn and raised it. She lived to be what, over fifteen years I believe."

Dave nodded.

"So, anyway...." Susie sipped her coffee and sat back, rubbing her gnarled hands together. "Back when it was about a year old or so, I came across a wounded buck while I was hiking the railroad tracks." She looked at the girls. "Don't worry, I saved him. But there weren't much life left in him at the time. I went and got my truck, and somehow by the grace of God, got him up and in the bed and off the tracks before the six o'clock train came along. I've taken care of just about every animal on earth. I even had a litter of skunks once. We don't see many skunk in these parts. I think the mom was a hitchhiker."

They all chuckled

"Have you had a lot of deer over the years?" Mindy asked.

"Oh yeah, probably thirty or forty."

"What happened to them all?"

"Happened to them? Well, most of them are still here. Some died of old age over the years. We have two hundred acres of mostly woods. They come and go when they want. They don't go far away."

The girls sat with big smiles. They couldn't have found a better place for their deer if they'd tried.

"Sadly though, there's going to come a time when we won't be able to take anymore. There's just too damned many deer everywhere. I can't feed them all. No one can feed them all."

"Do you believe in culling herds?" Yolanda asked. "You don't think that's the answer, do you?"

"Actually, I don't have a problem with culling herds, if the meat is needed and is going to be eaten. I have a problem with assholes who can't shoot straight. I have a problem with handing a gun to someone just because they can fill out an application. We don't put people behind the wheel of a car without first making sure they know how to drive, do we. Would they give a cop a gun without training? Or a soldier? Here, soldier, here's your gun, now go on out and aim it at someone." She paused to take another sip of her coffee. "Don't even get me started about bow hunting. I can't stand to see any animal suffer. There's got to be a better way."

Bethann glanced out the window; it had stopped snowing. It was one-thirty in the morning. "Susie, you have been so kind. We need to get out of here and let you get some sleep."

Susie looked at her. "Nah, don't worry about me. I took a nap earlier. But I'm thinking maybe you all need to get a little sleep and give the road department a chance to plow. Dave can check on your horse. You'ns just need to go in the living room and find yourself a place to lay down." She started clearing the dishes. Bethann helped her. The girls didn't need any coaxing; they took the cats and headed for a place to sleep. Mrs. Butchling, too.

"Susie, about Easy To Do?"

"He's yours, if you want him," she said.

"For how much? What are you selling him for?"

"Peace of mind," Susie said, with a snicker. "He's humbled me long enough."

"Well, at least let me pay you what you paid for him?"

Susie looked at her long and hard. "You have a pride thing, too. Don't you?"

Bethann smiled. "When did you say you bought him?"

"Last February. Now go on, go get some rest. I start chores at five."

"Good night," Big Dave said jovially, implying Susie knew best and she just might as well listen. "I'll give your horse some hay and water her."

Bethann phoned Benjamin to let him know they arrived safely, then burrowed down and fell asleep instantly. She dreamt she was in a castle with a thousand rooms, and in every room there was a deer. They all had plenty of room, plenty of food, but they were all lonely. In the courtyard below, there was a multitude of deer, herd upon herd upon herd without enough food who kept stepping on one another, and....

"Bethann." Mindy nudged her gently. "Susie has eggs made. It's time to wake up."

"What time is it?"

"Six fifteen. We helped with chores. We're gonna come during spring break and help with the lambing. The herd's out back. They love it here. Pixie Dust said so. Your horse is so pretty. Come on, it's time to go."

Bethann sat up quickly and reached for her cell phone. "Call Audra. See if she can feed for us."

"We already did. She's on her way. Sydney said it's still snowing, but not as bad."

Bethann rubbed the sleep from her eyes and smiled.

"We've got the truck warming up."

They'd thought of everything. She phoned Benjamin, told him they'd be leaving shortly, and went into the bathroom to wash up. A cat sat curled up on the clothesbasket. It was a tabby, and reminded her of Phoenix. When she picked him up, he started purring. She carried him with her to the kitchen. Susie looked up from the table and frowned. "Where'd he come from?"

"Uh...I don't know. He was in the bathroom."

"Well, he'd better be housebroken or he ain't staying."

Bethann laughed.

Susie had made a feast for breakfast, bacon, green eggs, thick sliced toast, home-churned butter and orange marmalade. They all joined hands and bowed their heads as Big Dave said grace. "Lord, we thank you for the food we are about to eat, and for new friends. Be with them as they journey home and guide them to safety. Amen."

"Amen."

They all ate until they were stuffed. Mrs. Butchling and Susie chatted up a storm. They were close in age, and had some of the same fond memories: favorite songs during high school, mohair sweaters, roller rinks, teased hair, and cars with tailfins. They all helped wash dishes, and were soon bundled up and heading out to the barn.

Bethann left a check on the coffee table; the sum of what Susie paid for Easy To Do, plus twelve months' board, and a note. When she got to the barn, the girls were saying good-bye to the deer. They all had tears in their eyes, but smiles on their faces. After all, they'd be back in a little over a month. That's if their mothers said it was okay - and knowing them, they'd probably already phoned to ask.

Mindy stroked the side of Pixie Dust's face. "Bye, little one. I'll miss you."

Becky wiped her eyes. "Me, too."

Yolanda gave her a hug. "Bye, Pixie Dust."

They told the rest of the herd good-bye and named each one of them so they would always be a part of their lives. They named them after Santa's reindeer. Susie smiled. Then they looked in on Belle and her fawns. The littlest one was Rudolph. He was standing and nursing, his twin nursing from the other side. They were all happy and content.

"Good-bye, we'll see you at Easter."

"Is there a church close by?" Becky asked.

"Oh yes," Big Dave said. He was a deacon.

It was time to load the horses. Mindy led Malaki out of her stall, and waited for Bethann and Easy To Do. Bethann stood looking in at him for a moment before entering his stall. She thought of Persian Sun. She thought of Leah Oliver. The past.... Was she doing the right thing? Had she made the right decision?

Easy To Do raised his head and nickered at her, erasing all doubts. "All right, come on," she said. She walked into his stall and put his halter on. "Let's get you home."

They loaded Malaki first and then Easy To Do. Both loaded without incident. When the stall partitions were put in place, the two horses facing one another, Malaki promptly stomped her foot and squealed at him. Easy To Do turned his head and gave her a sideways glance in response, as if to reply, "Okay, whatever you say." And they all laughed.

Susie picked up Leah Oliver's wool blanket and folded it neatly. She started to hand it to Bethann then, but hesitated. "Would you mind if I kept this?" she asked, running her hand over the wool fabric.

Bethann just looked at her. They all just looked at her.

"I don't know why I want it," Susie said. "God knows I've got enough blankets. But for some reason, I think I'm supposed to have it."

Tears welled up in Bethann's eyes. "Then it's yours," she said, and hugged her dearly. They all piled in the truck. Big Dave waved, standing next to Susie, his arm around her and her holding the blanket. The girls and Bethann and Mrs. Butchling waved good-bye. "See you soon," they said, and weren't five miles down the road when the CB crackled.

"This is Sassie Susie, come in Angels of Mercy, out."

"That's us!" Yolanda said. "This is the Angels of Mercy."

"Tell Bethann I said she didn't have to do this."

"Tell her I know," Bethann said.

With the snow having stopped and daylight, it made for an uneventful ride home. They stopped once at a roadside rest area to use the ladies room and Mrs. Butchling drove from there. Bethann glanced at her watch and then at her little sister. "With a little luck, you'll make your violin lesson."

Mindy chuckled. "Okay, Mom."

"Speaking of Mom, get her on the phone."

Mindy laughed, dialed the number, and handed her the phone. Bethann and her mom had a delightful conversation. "Everyone's fine, we just went out for breakfast. Yep, Mindy's eating well. Did she practice the violin? Yes, as a matter of fact she did. Love you, tell Dad. Bye-bye."

The girls fell asleep soon after that. Bethann looked over her shoulder at them and smiled. She was so proud of them. "They're good girls," Mrs. Butchling said. "I'm always afraid they're going to get hurt with their antics, but…."

Bethann had a feeling the next time she asked the girls what they were up to, they might not be so reluctant to tell her.

"You know, I've been thinking about what your father said about my life insurance policy."

Bethann looked at her.

"No matter what, I'm not selling Dew Drop. If I do end up going to the poor house, at least I'll have a ride."

Bethann nodded, knowing she'd feel the same way. "I'm so sorry about your husband."

"He was a good man. I miss him already," she said, and bit at her trembling bottom lip. "Oh, don't get me started."

Bethann smiled sadly. "I can't thank you enough."

"It was nothing. This is the most alive I've felt in quite a while. I've become rather paranoid lately."

"About what?"

"Everything. My job, my husband, my life…Dew Drop."

Bethann looked at her; now was the time. "Are you worried he doesn't get enough to eat?"

Mrs. Butchling shrugged.

"He does, he looks great. But if you want to feed him a little extra when you're there, go ahead."

"Thank you. I uh…."

Bethann patted her shoulder. Enough said about that. "Tell me though, have you been bringing the apples?"

Mindy opened her eyes.

"No." Mrs. Butchling shook her head.

"I told you it was Leah Oliver," Mindy said.

Bethann laughed. "Go back to sleep."

When they made the turn to start up the hill toward Maple Dale, it was to the prettiest snow they had ever seen. Every snowflake glistened in the sunlight. There were tire tracks leading down to the barn, one set obviously from Audra, and the other....

The county official's car was parked, waiting for them. They pulled down and around then back up to the front door of the barn. The man got out of his car and walked toward them.

"I'll do all the talking," Bethann said, which was okay with everyone else, because they certainly didn't want to.

"Ma'am." He tipped his hat. "Ya'll out awful early, now aren't ya?"

"We had to go get a horse," Bethann said. "What can I do for you?"

The girls and Mrs. Butchling went about the business of unloading the horses amidst the falling snow. Malaki whinnied and whinnied, the first to be led off the trailer. When Yolanda opened the barn doors, all the horses nickered and whinnied back. Patience, who was the loudest of all, was definitely happy to see Malaki.

Mrs. Butchling walked down the aisle way to greet Dew Drop and help Yolanda prepare another stall. Becky led Easy To Do off the trailer, just as calm as can be. He hesitated before going into the barn, tossing his head playfully and snorting as he looked around. Bethann smiled.

"Ma'am? Ma'am, are you listening?" He'd been talking about breaking the law and not doing anything stupid, and....

"No, I'm sorry. What did you say?"

The man looked at her. "Never mind. Ya'll have a nice day."

"You, too," Bethann said. She felt totally at peace as she followed her new horse into the barn. She was home. And for the first time ever, it felt like home.